inside
field hockey

for women

vonnie gros

Contemporary Books, Inc.
Chicago

Library of Congress Cataloging in Publication Data

Gros, Vonnie, 1935-
    Inside field hockey for women.

    Includes index.
    1. Field hockey.   I. Title.
GV1017.H7G76   796.35'5   79-50977
ISBN 0-8092-7216-4
ISBN 0-8092-7215-6

Published by Contemporary Books, Inc.
180 North Michigan Avenue, Chicago, Illinois 60601
Manufactured in the United States of America
Library of Congress Catalog Card Number: 79-50977
International Standard Book Number: 0-8092-7216-4 (cloth)
                                    0-8092-7215-6 (paper)

Published simultaneously in Canada by
Beaverbooks
953 Dillingham Road
Pickering, Onartio L1W 1Z7
Canada

contents

acknowledgments

A particular thanks to Mary Ann Porter and the late Jane Kennedy, who guided me through my high school years. A special thanks to Eleanor Snell whose competitive spirit and enthusiasm were way ahead of her time. She allowed and encouraged all of us at Ursinus to compete to the best of our abilities. A coach is only as good as the talent of the players she coaches. I am truly grateful for the enthusiasm of the players I've coached at Upper Darby High School, West Chester State College, Princeton University, and those from all over the country in our national program. Their willingness to experiment and push on with new ideas has always been my inspiration. Thanks to U.S.F.H.A. President Bea Toner, whose leadership and understanding of the times have guided field hockey very successfully into the U.S. Olympic program. Many thanks to Betty Tayes and Marilyn O'Neill, whose advice and patience were instrumental in writing and organizing my material. I am also most appreciative of Dorothy Heimgartner for preparing the manuscript and to Laurie Usher, Steve Gyrsting, Mike Cash, and Bonnie Caton for their photographic contributions.

Some of the leaders of the '70s: Liz Plummer, Gwen Cheeseman, Robin Cash, Diane Wright.

Two of the top players of the '60s: Gertie Dunn and Mary Ann Harris.

introduction

Field hockey is international in scope, being played by large numbers of men and women in many countries around the world. America is quite possibly the only country where it is predominantly a girls' and women's sport. Men play in some areas, but for the most part they are foreigners who are more or less reliving their playing days back in their homelands. Like most women's sports, before the inception of Title IX field hockey played a minor role on the American sports scene. Now it is played by some 65,000 players on the junior high, senior high, college, and club levels. It is a game that is simple in concept, involving continuous action, constant changes of ball possession, and the obvious objective of putting the ball in the opponents' goal.

Maneuvering the ball with a hooked stick both individually and in combination with teammates is the fun and challenge of the game. It is a sport for everyone, because size makes little or no difference in how well you play.

In the past, the U.S. was very loyal to the English system and style of play. Early pioneers of this style (Anne Townsend, Betty Shellenberger, and Libby Williams, among many others) were instrumental in setting a coaching and playing standard that was the backbone of American field hockey. During the '60s a new competitive athletic spirit emerged as women became "legitimate" sports participants. Winning became important. Players wanted more coaching, conditioning, and an improved selection process.

Could field hockey be social, competitive and fun? How much money should be spent on the players and the game? It was a time of confusion and controversy. The national teams reflected the times by having only a few players repeatedly selected. Gertie Dunn, Mary Anne Harris, Betty Miller, Adele Boyd, and I were the leaders who put the U.S. on the brink of international prominence. Our win/loss record did not improve that much, but we were more competitive and could no longer be easily dismissed, because our "scrappiness" on the field was a threat.

However, the greatest and most significant change in the game came in the '70s with the emergence of championships at every level and the inclusion of field hockey for women in the Olympics. The United States Field Hockey Association would have to develop the American game nationwide if we were to be competitive. Under the leadership of Bea Toner, the U.S.F.H.A. made some dramatic changes. The structure of the game became more flexible, administrative changes were made, and we took advantage of our own coaching strengths.

The U.S.F.H.A. has two commitments, and one is no good without the other. One is to make our national team as good as it can be so that we will be serious contenders for world and Olympic championships. The other is to increase the number of players and coaches at all levels, and thus improve the quality of the game. Sheer persistence and hustle could never consistently overcome the skillful techniques and tactics of England, Holland, or New Zealand. The few "big wins" or "moral victories" we won were often followed by losses to teams with less athletic talent. It was obvious that "psych" alone was not enough. The only things that win and are consistently reliable on a hockey field are well-executed ball-control techniques and tactics. Frenzied "hit-ahead-and-chase" and "rodeo hockey" simply do not work against equally determined but poised, skillful players. The principles of the new game are ball possession, poise, accuracy, concentration, and control—instead of rush, go, hit-it-ahead, and get-it-out. Heaps of flailing bodies and dust storms in the goalmouth, created by equal numbers of players trying to get the ball in or out of the goal, is unacceptable play. Efficiency on the hockey field is not frantic activity but composure, control with quickness. Now, a woman who plays field hockey effortlessly is not considered lazy.

If we are going to have good American players we must begin developing them at the grass roots level. The U.S.F.H.A. runs coaches' clinics and workshops, as well as developmental camps for players all over the country. Players of all ages, who dream of competing in national and international field hockey, can attend player-selection camps at various sites during the summer. The goals of the national coaching committee are to teach the techniques and tactics that are consistently required in women's field hockey, regardless of the variations in the arrangement of the players on the field.

The U.S.F.H.A. program and the college programs are proof that we are on the right track. Young players can eagerly look forward to playing collegiate field hockey almost anywhere in the country. In just four years the national collegiate tournament, organized by the Association of Intercollegiate Athletics for Women (A.I.A.W.), has produced balanced results. Also on the horizon is increased intra-hemispheric and world competition, and the ultimate athletic achievement— the Olympics. The modern stars of field hockey, like Julie Staver, Robin Cash, Beth Anders, Mikki Flowers, and Gwen

Cheeseman have set the stage for an American style of play. They have been the leaders of our significantly improved record on the international scene in the last few years. Because of them, and many unnamed others, a lot of twelve-to-fifteen-year-old girls will be playing in the XXIII Olympiad in Los Angeles in 1984.

I've competed in hundreds of games against the local, regional, and national women's field hockey teams of New Zealand, Australia, eastern and southern Africa, Europe, and Great Britain. The "hit-ahead-and-chase" style that worked in our American high school, college, club, and sectional games was neither successful nor respected by those talented foreign teams. I was very frustrated, because I felt we had athletic talent equal to or better than many of our opponents, but we obviously lacked the basic ball-control techniques and tactics necessary to win in international competition. Our players could not dribble past an opponent or receive a pass fast enough to keep possession of the ball. Our passing also lacked timing, pace, accuracy, and simplicity.

I have conducted field hockey clinics, taught at field hockey camps, and coached the national women's field hockey team of the United States. As a result of this experience, I am convinced that we must impress our young players with the importance of ball control. Understanding ball control will make women's field hockey a better game—and more fun to play and watch. I already see signs of improvement in our players. Coaches are now "undercoaching" young and inexperienced players, by giving them only the basic rules of field hockey before letting them play. As the young players gain experience, they are challenged to perfect the skills and tactics necessary to control the ball and the game.

This book is basically written for field hockey players, although coaches will also find it informative. Don't simply read this book once but refer back to it while perfecting your game. Coaches soon realize that they have to work as hard as their players. Coaches and players must work together to build a winning team.

The ideas expressed in this book are based on my playing and coaching experiences, conversations with world-class players and coaches, reading books by knowledgeable hockey writers, and studying soccer tactics that are applicable to field hockey. I empathize with the fears and doubts that coaches may feel about practicing a new style of play and coaching. The mistakes I made in coaching women's field hockey, and there were many, gave me clues for improvement and further growth. I found great truth in the saying, "Those who never fail, never try!" The player's reward for trying is the triumph she feels when she intelligently and successfully executes the techniques and tactics of women's field hockey.

Vonnie Gros

It sure feels good to win!

Chapter 1
THE GAME

Field hockey is played by 2 opposing teams of 11 players each. One of the players on each team is a goalkeeper. The playing field is usually 100 yards long and 60 yards wide. The object of the game is to score goals against the opposing team by putting the ball across their goal line. Putting the ball across the goal line is called a goal, and counts as one point. The winning team is the one that scores the greatest number of goals, or points, by the end of the game. Ties, so-called because neither team has scored more goals than the other, are often permitted in nonchampionship games. The length of a game may vary according to local custom or the level of play. Usually, 70 minutes of playing time is the *maximum* length of a single game (not including time-outs and other legal interruptions in the game).

Although many sports are competitive, with similar principles of movement and the need for physical and mental prepara-tion, each sport has its own characteris-tics. In field hockey this uniqueness cen-ters on the playing stick (used to move the ball around during the game) and the obstruction rule.

The playing stick looks roughly like a human leg—a long, straight shaft ending in a footlike hook, or toe. The stick is flat on the left side and the ball can only be struck with the flat side. This creates problems for a player, because she is usually stronger with the ball on her right side. However, coaches are now teaching players to use their sticks with the toes upside down, a technique called reverse sticks, with increasing success. The sec-ond unique characteristic of field hockey is the obstruction rule, which does not allow the player with the ball to protect or shield it. This rule is very important in forming a clear understanding of the way field hockey is played. In other sports, protecting the ball is taken for granted. Except for the playing stick and the rule

The player with the ball is violating the obstruction rule because she allowed the ball to get behind her. Instead of moving her feet, she reaches for the ball with her stick and uses her shoulders and hips to shield the ball from her opponent.

against obstruction, field hockey is tactically similar to soccer—the field hockey player moves a much smaller ball around the field with a stick.

Field hockey is a game that cannot be orchestrated from the bench because it is a game of constant movement, has limited substitutions, and very few set plays. However, players do have patterns of play that are determined by the situation at the moment, the area of the field, and the score. The 11 players attempt to put the ball in the opponents' goal while preventing the opponents from scoring goals against them. The 10 field players are basically divided into forwards, midfielders, and defenders. The goalkeeper has become a more mobile player, but her job is essentially the same as it has always been: to stop the opposition from scoring goals against her team. A whole chapter is devoted to her later.

FORWARDS

The forwards are the goal scorers. They need to develop excellent ball control,

speed, acceleration, and clever dribbling. The inside forwards must be opportunistic goal scorers. The wingers must carry the ball down the flank and pass it into

U.S. player Sheryl Johnson is about to "pull the trigger" and shoot for the goal.

scoring position. The right winger, in particular, can be invaluable in setting up a score because she can easily and quickly pass left. Wingers must keep the game play wide by maintaining their wing position. Inside forwards must move well without the ball. All forwards must tackle the opposing defenders when they lose the ball.

MIDFIELDERS

Midfielders, or link players, are the key to the game. They play attack (offense) and defense, so excellent physical fitness is an absolute must. They must be strong tacklers who understand their role in the team's defensive organization. On attack they are the playmakers who appear to thread a needle in penetrating the opponents' defense. They must be able to change the point of attack and not allow the ball to become bogged down on one side. They provide depth to the attack by moving up behind the forwards in position for a back pass. In addition, they must be good give-and-go players. Teams should, if possible, have a balance of strength in their midfielders. If two midfielders are used, one should be defense-oriented and the other attack-oriented. If the midfielders break down in their linking of the attack and defense, the team will lose effectiveness.

DEFENDERS

Backs

These players predominantly play defense and must be able to play man-to-man defense. The right and left backs, or wingbacks, mark the opposing wings. They must be both strong interceptors and tacklers. They must be constantly aggressive. They must be alert to a possible breakaway and prepared to move in and tackle a dangerous forward or to back up

the goalkeeper moving out of the goal to face a dangerous attacker. Solid, constructive, confident clearing of opponents from the defensive end of the field is necessary. Sometimes the backs should join the attack or a counterattack. The center back does the same things as the wingback, but she faces the opponents' most dangerous inside forward. The center back rarely attacks.

Sweeper

This player supports the backs by always being in position to intercept a ball passed through the defense, or to meet an opposing attacker with the ball who breaks through the backs. The sweeper must have the speed to get to loose balls first. She must be aggressive enough to run for the loose ball, but smart enough to know when not to take unnecessary chances. If the sweeper doesn't track down a loose ball, then the backs will wear themselves out chasing the ball. Because the sweeper is free as an extra defender, she is the leader of the defense and should direct her defenders with specific instructions, not just idle chatter. She must know where everyone is in relation to the ball. It is a real plus if the sweeper is tall because reach can be vital in the defending area.

SYSTEMS

System, or the arrangement of players on the field, is highly overrated as a formula for winning. Tactics are what make things happen. That's why two teams playing a 4-2-3-1 pattern may play it differently, because each coach sees things a little differently. No system will overcome technical failure or inaccurate passing or shooting. Teams that play systems win, not so much because of the formation of players, but because they execute techniques and tactics well. They pass accu-

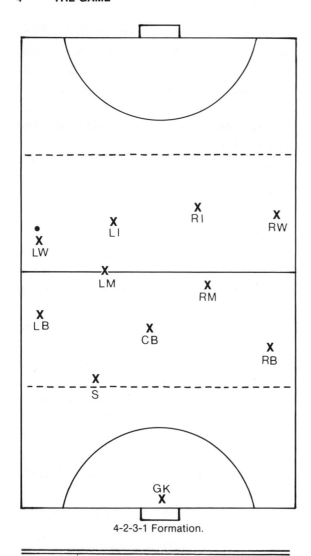

4-2-3-1 Formation.

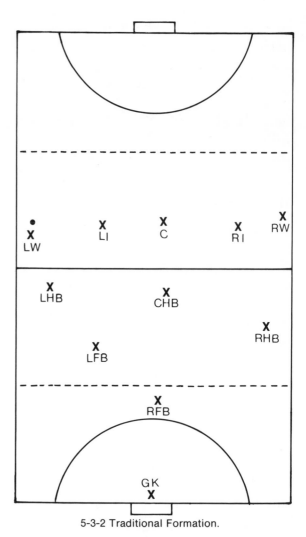

5-3-2 Traditional Formation.

Key to Systems Diagrams

LW = Left winger (forward)
RW = Right winger (forward)
LI   = Left inside forward
RI   = Right inside forward
LM = Left midfielder
RM = Right midfielder
CM = Center midfielder
LB   = Left back
RB   = Right back
CB   = Center back
S   = Sweeper
GK = Goalkeeper
C   = Center
LFB = Left full-back
RFB = Right full-back
LHB = Left half-back
RHB = Right half-back
CHB = Center half-back

rately, they change their point of attack, they play team defense. In general, they perform all the individual and team movements well. When teams changed from the traditional 5-3-2 formation they often ran into trouble offensively, because the new game requires team work, particularly in passing. The midfielders must definitely be used in the passing patterns, both among themselves and in combination with forwards. There is a tendency for a defender to gain possession of the ball and immediately send it to the forward, who goes straight to the goal. If any consideration is given to back passing, it usually follows a pause or hesitation and is done timidly—consequently, it

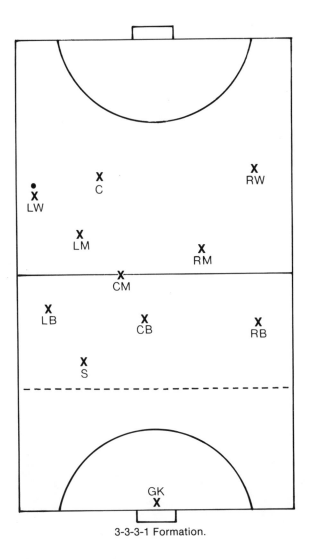

3-3-3-1 Formation.

is useless. Thus, ball possession to such players is still only a theory, not something to actually practice in a game. It takes time for players to become comfortable. Freshmen will be good when they are seniors, if they and their coaches are patient.

Team formations (like 4-2-3-1) are usually written and discussed with the first number (4 in this case) indicating forwards, the second number (2 in this case) indicating midfielders, the third number (3 in this case) indicating backs, and the last number (1 in this case) indicating the sweeper(s), if any. Most authorities agree that a minimum of 4 defenders, 2 midfielders, and 3 forwards is necessary in modern field hockey. The goalkeeper's position is inflexible and is not included in the formation. Since the formation must total 10 players (without the goalkeeper), that leaves 1 player to "fudge" with. The position she assumes will depend on the talents of her teammates and the strategy necessary to compete against other teams.

West Chester State College 1976 National Collegiate Champions in full uniform.

Chapter 2
FIELDS, EQUIPMENT, UNIFORMS

FIELDS

For a variety of reasons field markings and conditions may have to be modified. When this occurs the essential regulation markings will be the 16-yard circles, 7-yard penalty stroke mark, 25 yards between goal line and the 25-yard line (25 yards in front of each goal line), and the two 5-yard markings on the goal line (measured from each goalpost). Goal lines and striking-circle lines must be 3 inches wide. The white spot, 7 yards straight out from the center of the goal line must be no more than 6 inches in diameter. The front of the goalposts must touch the outer edge of the goal line. Flags must be flexible and nonmetallic to avoid injury.

The characteristics of a good field include a level area with quality grass, less than 1 inch high. The field needs fertilizing, aerating, watering, and cutting at the appropriate times of the year. Cutting and watering during the summer months is particularly important. Players deserve to play on a surface where technique and skill are not just a lottery because of constant bad bounces.

Playing Areas of the Field

Playing areas of the field are referred to frequently throughout the book. The boundaries are approximate and may vary slightly from coach to coach. The natural breakdown of the field appears to be the 25-yard line but I feel that confines the attack and defense areas too much. Within this area umpires can award penalty corners (a hit, flick, or push of the ball awarded to the attacking team, made from the defending team's goal line, at least 10 yards to the side of either goalpost) against defenders who flagrantly and/or deliberately foul an opponent. An attack area for one team is obviously a defense area for the other.

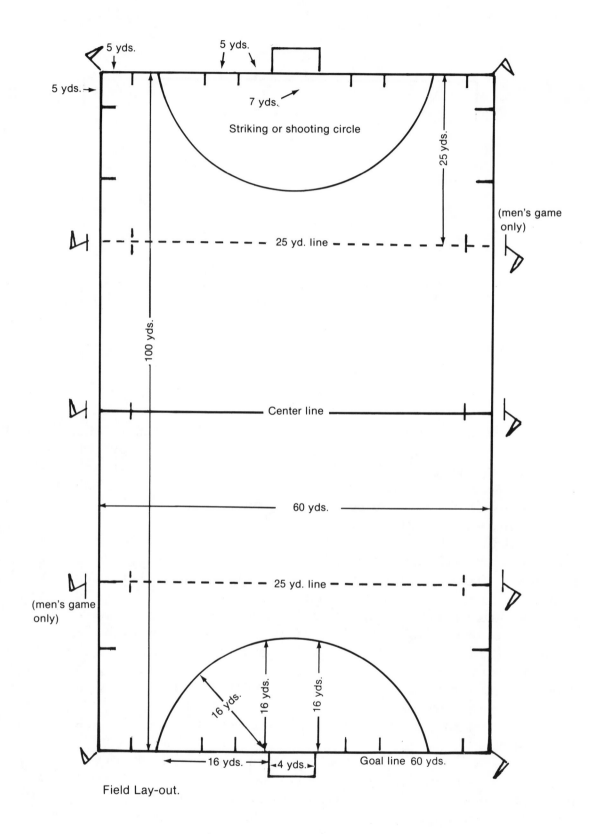

Field Lay-out.

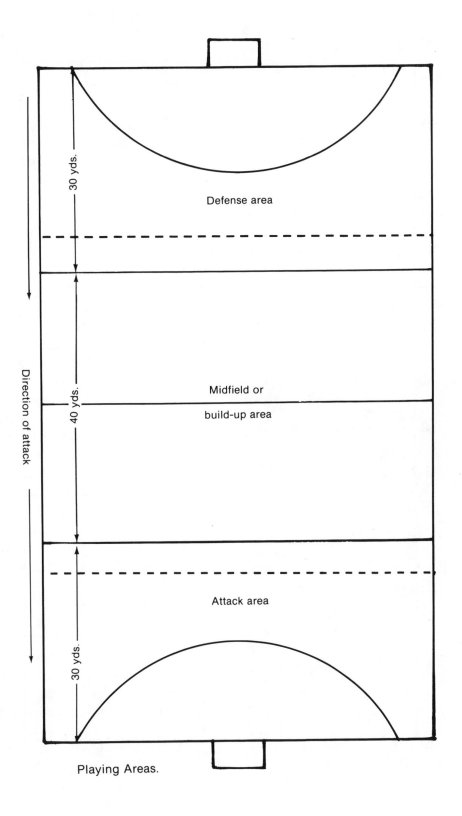

Playing Areas.

FIELD PLAYERS' EQUIPMENT

Sticks

The 4 factors to consider in selecting a playing stick are weight, length, stiffness, and balance. These 4 qualities combine to give the stick its "feel." The stick must be comfortable and easily manipulated. Comfort begins with a thin but strong handle. This thin handle allows for a better distribution of weight into the head (toe) of the stick. The Regina is the first stick in this country to come out with a polyfiber that is wrapped around the handle of the stick so it can be made thin without losing strength. It is also reasonably priced.

When you swing the stick, the weight in the head should feel heavy without being unwieldy, giving the stick a balanced feeling. To get a good feel of the stick, move the head over an imaginary ball as in dribbling. The handle should be stiff but not rigid. Stiffness allows for greater feeling for the ball when receiving or dribbling because the feel is not concealed by the flexibility of the stick. A stiff stick also allows for greater force when hitting, pushing, and flicking, and gives added strength in gaining possession of the ball when struggling with an opponent. Avoid playing with sticks that were stiff when new but become too flexible when broken in.

The length of the stick for most high school, college, and club players should be 35 to 36 inches. Only on very rare occasions should you use a 37-inch stick. Junior high and short players need 30 to 34-inch sticks, referred to as junior sticks. The weight of sticks may be indicated in ounces or referred to as very light (VL), light (L), medium (M), and heavy (H). Very light sticks are 16 to 17 ounces, light sticks are 18 ounces, medium sticks are 19 to 20 ounces, and heavy sticks are 21 ounces and over. However, blind selection of weights, particularly of unfamiliar sticks, is a mistake because distribution of weight is most important. When the stick's weight is in a thick handle, balance and comfort are lost.

Another consideration in selecting a stick is the strength and width of the splice, the area where the handle joins the blade. Also, the grain in the mulberry head must be close, long, and even, to reduce the chance of splintering. The grip may be toweling, rubber, or leather. The choice is basically a personal matter but the most important factor is to avoid grips that come unraveled quickly at the top.

Players choosing sticks must consider the needs of their playing positions. Those who must hit hard over long distances need heavier sticks. Those who

Force will be lost in the push pass when the stick has this much flexibility.

primarily push, flick, and need deft stick-work should use a lighter stick for quickness and maneuverability. Proper care of a stick calls for periodic application of linseed oil on the mulberry head and proper storage. Avoid storing your stick in very dry places.

Shinguards

Leg protection should be made compulsory by the coach. It is foolish to suffer pain from being struck by a ball or stick on the shinbone when there are very light, comfortable shinguards that can easily be inserted into the socks. Some are made from a foam rubber substance which is built right into stirrup socks. The standard plastic guards that come with or without ankle protection are also readily available.

Tooth Protectors

Plastic guards similar to those worn by football players are most frequently used.

GOALKEEPER'S EQUIPMENT

The goalkeeper must be able to trust her protective equipment since she won't play well if every shot causes pain. She must always be warm without losing mobility and agility.

Legs

The legs can be protected with canvas or cane pads. Canvas pads have been very popular for years because they are light, comfortable, and less expensive. It is usually necessary to add padding at crucial spots. The advantage of the cane pads is that they present a broad, square front to

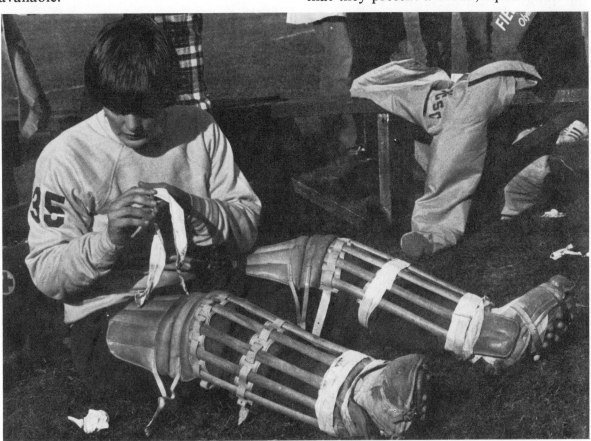

Goalkeeper is well-protected with these cane pads reinforced by padded rolls and canvas kickers with leather overboot. *Photo by Laurie Usher.*

shots, so that any shot that hits the pads will not deflect into the goal. Cane pads provide excellent protection because they are reinforced by padded rolls. Of course, they are also more expensive and heavier.

Feet

The canvas kicker, which needs added padding, is light and allows for instep kicking only. The leather overboot very rarely requires more protection. It has a strong, reinforced flat front that allows a strong toe kick in addition to the instep kick. If the canvas kicker is used, cleated shoes with reinforced toecaps should be worn because these kickers are attached by straps under the shoe and behind the heel. The overboot is built for the front of the foot to be inserted. The underside of the boot is cleated, so the shoes used should have removable cleats that are taken out of the front of the shoe. The heel cleats remain in place.

Hands

The goalkeeper needs to protect the back of her hands and forearms, as well as the palms of her hands when she is stopping aerial balls (primarily with her left hand in field play, and with both hands on a penalty stroke). Gauntlet-type gloves, like those worn by male lacrosse players, are the best, even though some light padding may be needed in the palm. The gloves must not have webbing between the fingers.

Chest

It is unusual to see a goalkeeper wearing a chest protector. Those who do wear them use a softball catcher's pad or lacrosse goalkeeper's protector.

Face

To protect the face the goalkeeper must wear a form-fitting mask, usually plastic without protrusions that could be danger-

ous. Although few goalkeepers now wear them, I think more will be wearing them in the near future.

Goalkeeper wears a mask similar to the ice hockey goalkeeper's mask.

Stick

For ease of handling, the goalkeeper's stick should be very light and shorter than one which would be used on the field.

TEAM EQUIPMENT

Balls

Every team needs two balls per person. This allows for one-ball-one-player drills, and pressure drills at the same time. Balls are generally plastic for practice and leather for games. Qualities needed are durability, cleanability, and playability. In the past finding a ball with these qualities at reasonable cost was the biggest problem. Now, for the first time an American company, Penn Monto, is making a ball at a reasonable price that does have the required qualities.

Goals and Nets

Lightweight, portable goals with legal posts, crossbars, and backboards are readily available. Netting must be securely fastened to the frame.

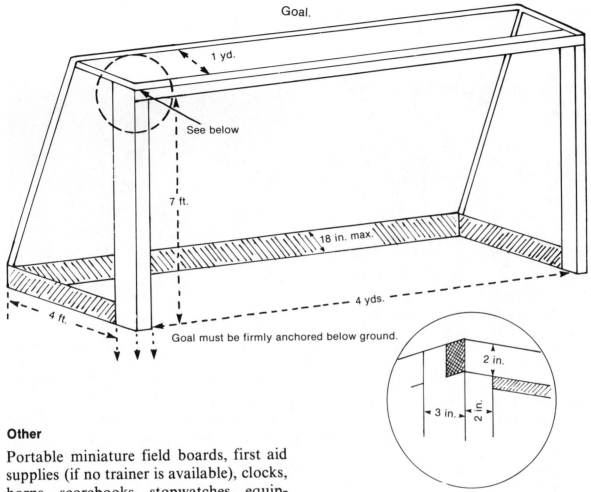

Goal.

1 yd.

See below

7 ft.

18 in. max.

4 yds.

4 ft.

Goal must be firmly anchored below ground.

2 in.

3 in.

2 in.

Other

Portable miniature field boards, first aid supplies (if no trainer is available), clocks, horns, scorebooks, stopwatches, equipment bags, water vehicles, and whistles are all needed.

UNIFORMS

Game

Kilts are worn in the traditional Eastern bastions of field hockey. Lately, pleated kilts are being replaced by reversible wraparounds, with two distinct colors on either side. These are very practical because they are easily adjusted, are two uniforms in one, and cost the same price with some manufacturers as the pleated kilts. Some teams are more comfortable in shorts, particularly in the West. Shorts are certainly acceptable, but care should be taken on the fit and/or type of material, to avoid a binding effect when players are fully extended during a game.

Shirts can be long sleeved or short sleeved. They are made of nylon, rayon, and cotton mixtures. Raglan sleeves are preferred to allow freedom of motion. Players should not be distracted by ill-fitting shirts. More and more, numbers are becoming mandatory on shirts for identification purposes.

Socks can be regular knee socks, tube socks, or stirrup socks.

The goalkeeper must look like her team. In cold weather she must be warm, so sweat pants are advisable. I recommend that the goalkeeper wear sweat or warm-up pants all the time, because she is likely to feel more comfortable if her leg pad straps don't come in direct contact with her skin.

When legs and feet work like this, strong, comfortable shoes that give ample support and grip are absolutely essential.

Practice

Practices cannot be fully effective if there are many colors on the field, even with pinnies! Coaches must have an appropriate number of scrimmage vests and stirrup socks in two colors. Scrimmage vests are very light and pull on easily. Stirrup socks can be put on over the shoe and they hold up amazingly well. They can also be pulled over sweat pants on cold days. If high schools or colleges don't provide practice uniforms, the players must be told not to wear the colors of the vests or socks.

Shoes

Probably nothing can cause more discomfort to the player than shoes. Part of the problem is that cleated shoes are not yet made for a woman's foot. Women must experiment with the variety of men's cleated shoes available to find the one that fits best. She wants a snug fit but also needs the comfort, lightness, and flexibility that is provided in the shoe's material, padded backs, padded tongues, and padded Achilles tendon supports. Shoes cost from $15 to $40 a pair and big name brands cost upwards of $40.

Field hockey is a series of hundreds of often dramatic struggles between two or more opponents for possession of the ball. *Photo by Laurie Usher.*

Chapter 3
BASIC TACTICS

This is the most important chapter in the book because it explains the crux of winning and losing in field hockey. The biggest challenge facing field hockey coaches and players today is understanding the basic tactics and techniques of the game. Since the introduction of the "new" game in 1974, all persons associated with field hockey were convinced that their successes and failures were the result of reorganizing the 10 field players in patterns other than the traditional 5-3-2 formation. There is no denying that the arrangement of players on the field was changed, but the main emphasis, then and now, is on technique and tactics, especially tactics. Offensive play (team with the ball) and defensive play are more important than the position of players on the field. Keeping possession of the ball and regaining possession of the ball are purposeful, decisive, and cooperative work achieved by all team members. The era has ended when one player hits the

ball towards the goal, regardless of accuracy, and is followed by a teammate who dutifully chases the ball, hoping desperately that the opposition will miss it. Players are now taught to "read" the game. It is necessary to know where other players are on the field, and to anticipate what will develop next. It is not enough to simply know where the ball is.

Field hockey is a series of hundreds of often dramatic struggles, among two or more opponents, for possession of the ball. Tactics, executed with excellent techniques, win these battles. If you win most of these little battles, you will win the game. Tactics, therefore, include everything needed to win. They are everything that is important in attack and defense and the change from one to the other (called the transition). Tactics are the thinking and decision-making level in field hockey—the methods of constantly outwitting the individual opponent, or a group of opponents. Good tactics and

Player is straight dribbling with her head up to view the field and look for a teammate. *Photo by Mike Cash.*

sound techniques beat opponents. Techniques have team value only when they are executed with accuracy, timing, and speed, with each player aware of the placement of teammates and opponents alike on the playing field.

Tactical decisions cannot be made without vision. The player dribbling freely must lift her head often to view the whole field. Under pressure she must also use peripheral vision to view the action on all sides of her, while focusing on the immediate vicinity of the ball. For a player without the ball, it is much more important to watch the other players than to just follow the ball. Decisions are based on these observations. The concept of "space is time" is crucial. Time gives the player with the ball the opportunity to take advantage of the available options

and to move the ball accurately. In order to get the ball and have this time, a player has to find the best free space when she does not possess the ball. To find free space, players without the ball have to look around and move away from their opponents. Coordinating the moment of getting free with the hit or push of the ball by another player is the timing that makes passing work.

OFFENSIVE TACTICS

The attack begins the moment any player on the team gains possession of the ball. The team wants to complete a series of passes until a shot at the goal is possible. Successful attacks, regardless of formation, have several common principles. All these principles are designed to create and use space:

Player is breaking away from her opponent into the free space ahead of her. By using peripheral vision, she knows, even before getting the ball, that she has teammates upfield, one to the right and one to the left.

1. Getting free—A player moves away from an opponent into available space to receive the ball. By getting free this player should know, in advance, what she will do with the ball.

2. Playing without the ball—This is decoy running, where a player moves in order to open a space for a teammate who receives the ball.

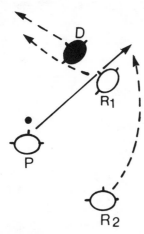

Decoy Run: Receiver₁ moves diagonally, taking her defender with her. Receiver₂ moves into vacated space to receive the pass.

These first two principles of purposeful running are often referred to as mobility.

3. Combination Playing—Two or three players passing in varying directions, long or short, and/or with different speeds. The objective is to change the point of attack to get an opposing defender out of position so that a sudden, penetrating pass can be made. Of primary importance is pulling defenders wide. Players must move out to spread the defense from sideline to sideline. One of the most obvious mistakes on the transition from defense to attack is to immediately move downfield towards the goal line, instead of moving to the sideline. Combination playing must also include depth—a player available for a back pass. The patience to hold back, rather than move the ball forward against an organized defense, will pull defenders toward you, leaving space behind them. When the defense is disorganized or outnumbered, a swift counter-

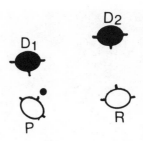

Receiver is providing neither width nor depth enough to successfully receive the pass.

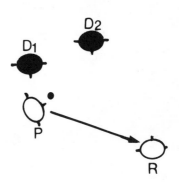

By moving away and back slightly, thus allowing sufficient width and depth, the receiver can now safely receive a pass.

attack must be made in which the ball is passed and dribbled forward before the defense can recover. This is equivalent to the fast break in basketball.

4. Improvisation—This is useful when talented players can, at the right moment, put a little "pizazz" into the game (in the attacking third of the field) with clever dribbling against one or two foes in combination or not. The result should be a good shot and a goal.

5. Scoring—There is only one statistic that really counts: which team scores the most goals. The previous 4 principles are very important aspects of all attacking patterns as long as they consistently result in penetrating the defense into the circle for good shots at the goal.

Possession of the ball has switched to the team in white. The attack begins immediately; the team who lost the ball is now on defense.

DEFENSIVE TACTICS

Defense is the opposite of attack. It attempts to deny space. As soon as the ball is lost the whole team is on defense. Players with specific defensive responsibilities must retreat to be part of an organized defensive unit, while the nearest forwards work to recover the ball. Effective defenses, whether player-to-player zone, or a combination, have common principles:

1. Pressure—The opponent with the ball is confronted in such a manner that she will be dispossessed, made to lose control, or forced to pass inaccurately. The ball should always be pressured. By doing so the other principles are easier to execute.
2. Marking—This is playing an opponent who doesn't have the ball but is a potential receiver. The marker must be where she can see both her opponent and the ball. As soon as the ball is

passed she must decide to intercept the ball or "tackle" her opponent immediately. A good marker is able to stay with a mobile attacker.

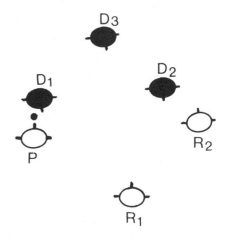

Defender$_1$ is pressuring the ball. Defender$_2$ marks, preventing Receiver$_2$ from receiving a pass. Defender$_3$ covers them both. If the ball gets through Defender$_1$ and Defender$_2$, whether dribbled or passed, the cover Defender$_3$ must challenge while the beaten defenders recover.

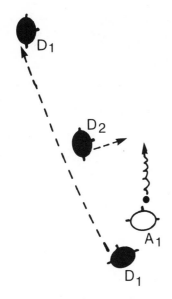

Defender₁ is beaten by Attacker₁. Defender₂ must cautiously take her until Defender₁ recovers and is in a covering position.

3. Covering—If the ball or a player with the ball gets past the defenders who are pressuring and marking, there must be other defenders to pick them up, as shown in the diagram at left. This defensive depth, or cover, must be close enough to intercept a pass that penetrates the first line of defenders, but not so close that one pass would eliminate 3 defenders who are covering in depth.

4. Recovery Run—When a player is beaten she must turn immediately and run to a covering position, while the previous covering player confronts and delays the player with the ball.

5. Restraint and Delay—Defenders cannot leave the organization of the defense and wildly charge at the player with the ball. Equally important is the cautious pressure that a defender must exert when the defense is disorganized and/or outnumbered. The latter is characterized by blocking the attacker's passing angles and slowing down and containing the ball carrier to buy time until defensive help arrives.

It's the final pass that goes past the goalkeeper and scores a goal.

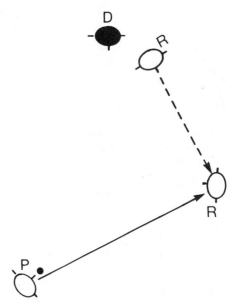

Chapter 4
PASSING TECHNIQUES AND TACTICS

Because passing techniques and tactics are so vital to the successful execution of a field hockey game, I will devote this entire chapter to them. Passing means intentionally moving the ball from one teammate to another. It is planned, deliberate, and the result of repeated practice. It is not luck. It is not based on hope. Good technique does not make good passes. Good passes result when technique is combined with timing, accuracy, pace, and knowledge of where players are on the field. Successful passes not only retain ball possession, they go past opponents and eliminate them. After an attacker penetrates the shooting area, her final pass goes by the goalkeeper and scores a goal!

Players of mediocre talent who willingly accept the challenge of ball control via passing will succeed consistently against faster opponents who just hustle while playing "hit-ahead-and-chase!" No amount of physical work can overcome

Going back and out to receive a pass is a frequent move by the wings.

consistent, precision passing. Intelligent, frequent, and varied passing means the ball is working and the ball never gets tired! The teams that control the ball for 4 to 6 passes at a time with no opponent able to get it will generally be able to win.

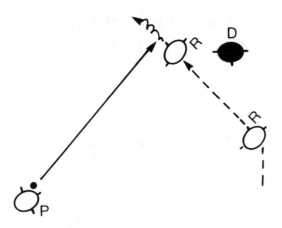

Square Pass: Receiver lags behind Passer (horizontally) because she must take the ball while running.

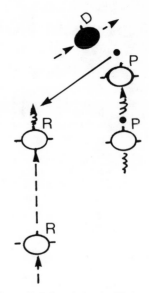

Back Pass: Receiver is back 45° from dribbler. She can receive back pass safely and then distribute ball elsewhere or give the ball back to first ball carrier. This is supporting the ball.

Diagonal Pass: Receiver breaks past Defender (either behind or in front of her) to safely receive.

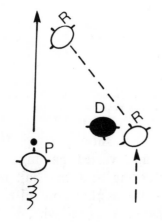

Through Pass: The ball is passed parallel to the sideline, past Defender.

Passing is the essence of teamwork. Generally speaking the player with the ball should have a choice of 3 players to pass to. These should be the nearest players ball side, on the side of the field where the ball is, where the players on the other side (weak side) are making or preparing a break toward the goal. The role of the passer, or player with the ball, and of the receiver, or player without the ball, will be examined carefully in the following paragraphs.

PLAYER WITH THE BALL

This player must find the open player and "hit" her with the pass. The passer must make sure no opponent is in or near the path of the pass to intercept the ball. The direction of the pass is determined by the target player or receiver. The passer must judge her receiver's speed if she is running so that the receiver takes the ball without a break in stride. There are times when the passer should hold the ball to give her teammate a little extra time to get free. She must do this even when teammates or enthusiasts on the sidelines are yelling at her to get rid of the ball.

Timing the pass is essential. Some players develop timing naturally and others have to be taught, although they will never be as consistently effective as the player who does it instinctively. A pass made too soon is never received. A pass made too late is intercepted. Timing is determined by correctly judging the positions of teammates and opponents.

Timing is important. The passer must correctly judge the position of teammates and opponents. In this case the pass will surely be intercepted.

The pass is received because the passer kept the ball until the moment when Receiver₂ was free to receive and the passer is close enough to the defenders that the pass will get through them before they have time to react.

Putting the proper speed on the ball is necessary for the success of a pass. The ball must be soft enough for the receiver to handle it without undue difficulty, but hard enough to reach the receiver without being intercepted.

Another factor is simplicity. The simple pass pays the greatest dividends. Far too many players try to do too much, or try to do the difficult or the spectacular. The passer should seldom overlook the obvious pass.

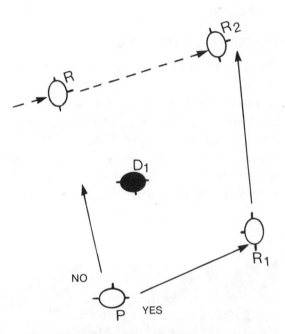

The simple and obvious pass to Receiver₁ will successfully move the ball upfield with a second, safe pass from Receiver₁ to Receiver₂.

Finally, the passer should mask her intentions until the last second, to convince the opponents that she's going to do one thing while, in fact, she plans to do another. Faking or disguising one's intentions makes it difficult for the defenders to anticipate where the ball is going.

Common Faults in Passing:

1. Passing behind the receiver because of lack of concentration on the movement of the receiver.

2. Releasing the ball automatically without judging the position of teammates or opponents.
3. Timidity in making the short pass—making it too soft.
4. Topping the ball on the short pass resulting from a lift of the head.
5. Failure to make the easy pass.
6. Giving away your intention by running 5 or 6 yards looking in the direction and/or allowing the stick to face the direction in which you intend to pass the ball.

PLAYER WITHOUT THE BALL

Playing without the ball, or getting free, is one of the most important parts in the game of field hockey. It is a matter of teamwork—your willingness to run to get the ball or to decoy defenders (drawing defenders toward you so that another teammate can receive the ball). Players who will happily work the entire game,

knowing they can't possibly get the ball every time, are true team players who often don't get the recognition they deserve. Put a superbly skilled player on a field with 10 "statues" and see how well she plays alone!

"Getting free" is a cliché heard a lot these days. Although some players do this instinctively, most players need instruction in order to move purposefully and decisively without the ball. Learning to watch the players, not just the ball, will help you decide when and where to move without the ball. The initiative for successful passing is taken by the player without the ball. One of the significant advances in field hockey team play is the ability of players to make decisions based on "player watching" and not "ball watching." Players begin to be player watchers when they start lifting their heads and moving into a good position away from the immediate action. De-

Ball-watching!

pending on where the nearest defender is, they move out, back, or up into a good field position. One of the criticisms of the "new" hockey played in America today is that the ball stays on one side of the field. This is because everyone is a ball watcher, so that the receiver always sends the ball back in the same direction from which she received it and, consequently, the point of attack never changes. If link players, center halves, and center backs in particular would lift their heads and look to the opposite side of the field from the ball, they would know in advance that when they receive the ball they can open the game with a cross-pass.

An important habit that should be cultivated early is to move into open space immediately after making a pass. By making a positive change of position an opportunity to receive a return pass is created. This is the basis of combined play and is particularly effective between backs and midfielders. For this to be successful, the first step must be quick and the first 5 yards must be rapidly gained.

Common Faults in Moving without the Ball:

1. Ball watching to the extent that players don't move until after the ball is hit or pushed.
2. Running for the sake of running, without checking the position of opponents and other teammates.
3. Standing still or drifting after making a pass.

SUPPORT

This is an aspect of team play that puts two attackers in the immediate vicinity of the ball against one defender. Possession is assured and easy, because a simple pass is all that is needed to the nearest team-

Player in white long pants is the supporting player. Because of the angle of the approaching defender the support player should be a little more forward.

mate. She has a broader visual field than the player with the ball who is probably being pressured. This player comes from behind quickly to receive a pass and is able to pass forward or change direction. The distance of the support player from her teammate is 8 to 12 yards in the midfield area. The distance in the attack area of the field could be less. The position of the support player is generally 45° behind her teammate, but the important thing is to be able to receive the ball without interference, and to be able to change the point of attack or to pass upfield. The only time the support player moves ahead of the player with the ball is when her teammate is not being pressured and does not need help.

PASSING PATTERNS

A passing pattern will not win a game by itself, although the first time a passing pattern is successfully executed is significant. A fluid, continuous combination of passing patterns without a pause, culminating in a goal, is the ultimate objective of the game.

Setting-up Pass

The setting-up passes are necessary when the defense is fully organized and ready. These are passes between backs and midfielders, midfielders and forwards, and forwards and backs. You must wait patiently for an opportunity to make a sudden penetrating lead pass to a breaking forward who will drive a shot at the goal. When backs and midfielders are always passing up to forwards the defense can deal with them easily. Interpassing and good support between links and backs often appears to be passing for its own sake, but defenders begin to make physical and/or mental errors if an opposing team retains possession of the ball for a long period of time.

Give and Go

The give and go pattern of play should be seen frequently all over the field. It is a primary example of pass and move. A player gives the ball to a teammate, quickly moves upfield behind the defender, and receives a return pass from her teammate. One of the elements that make it work is the "giving" player, who must draw the defender close enough before passing and then run past the defender on her blind side. The support (receiving) player must be close enough to get the pass quickly, and then must immediately return the ball behind the defender. This has a definite rhythm of 1–2 passing. If you break the rhythm or pause, it won't work.

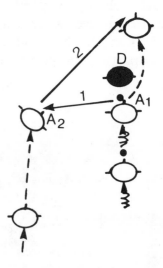

Give and Go.

Scissors

The scissors move is best done between two forwards, particularly when they have received a long upfield pass and could not possibly expect support from a midfield player. The player with the ball dribbles it at an angle against the defender. In the meantime, her teammate moves behind her. The defender is faced with the dilemma of the dribbler beating her, or a pass to the player cutting behind her. The success of the scissors is the ability of the dribbler to be a genuine threat by masking her intentions until the last minute. The pass, if made, must be quick and lateral or slightly forward. The receiver must time her run with the dribbler taking on the defender, so that she will take the pass while moving.

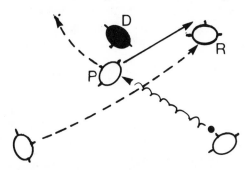

Scissors. Player with the ball dribbling diagonally may now choose either to pass to the open receiver or to fake a pass and keep the ball. Player without ball must go behind player with the ball to avoid obstruction.

Overlap

This is a move similar to the scissors in its timing and direction. However, the second player is a wingback coming down the sideline in a slightly curved run overlapping the wing who has the ball and is taking it at an angle toward the opposing back. Although the wingbacks don't do this very often in a game, when it does happen it offers an element of surprise that will penetrate the opposing defense when properly executed.

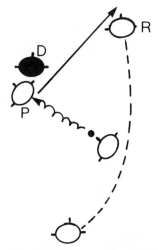

Overlap. Here the player, usually a link player or wingback, moves up from behind the player with the ball who is dribbling diagonally to be in a good receiving position in the vacated space.

In all the passing patterns described, the player with the ball is taking on a defender and should at times fake the pass and move on with the ball herself. The ability to proceed 1-on-1 against a defender makes the passing game that much more valuable.

U.S. Captain Julie Staver is shown maneuvering the ball through a web of Southern California opponents at a national tournament. *Photo by Laurie Usher.*

Chapter 5
OTHER TECHNIQUES AND TACTICS

The player who can dominate, maneuver, and master her stick and the ball is technically very sound. The truly skilled player, however, is one who knows when to use her techniques for the greatest benefit to her team. A player who technically hits a perfect ball, but hits too hard, with poor direction, and at the wrong time, is not skillful because her hit was of no value to the team. These decisions of timing, pace, and accuracy require good observation of the position of opponents and teammates on the field.

A typical action sequence in a field hockey game might go like this: You have the ball. No teammate is ready. You dribble forward. Here comes a defender. Should you pass? How close to the defender should you be before passing? No teammate is open. You have to go on your own past the defender. On what side should you beat her? Is she moving? How fast? You beat her. Should you pass or keep on going on your own? This is the

judgment a ball carrier needs to supplement her technique of dribbling. Her decisions are based on what she sees and on the success her actions will bring her team. There are some very technically sound players who cannot or will not work and make decisions that are necessary for team success. There are also players who read the total situation so well that a goal or shot will surely result, but they lack the technique to make it work. One is surely no good without the other.

In this chapter, I will discuss the techniques of dribbling and tackling. Following each technique, I will show their tactical uses in the game.

DRIBBLING TECHNIQUES

Dribbling is advancing the ball from one part of the field to another without the help of any teammates. It is the ability to control the ball until a teammate is free, or to go past (or beat) an opponent and then pass to a teammate who is in a better position than you are. Sometimes it means going alone beating an opponent or two and then scoring or at least getting a good shot at the goal. Dribbling and beating opponents should be saved for the attacking third of the field. Dribbling and passing is best for midfield play.

It cannot be emphasized enough that this technique should be learned with minimal instruction at first. As long as no rules are broken you should be as imaginative as possible as you move the ball around the field at random. You need to develop a feel for the ball on your stick. Changes of speed, direction, and stick and body fakes may come naturally to some players. Such players are natural forwards. Players, particularly young ones, get bored when they don't touch the ball enough. So hitting, receiving, tackling, and pushing should only be learned after dribbling.

When you hold the stick for the dribble the left hand comes onto the stick from above, with the right hand taking the stick from the right side about 4 inches to 6 inches below the left hand. The position of the left hand in this manner freely allows the use of reverse stick when dribbling in a zigzag fashion. When the stick is in the dribbling position, the back of the left hand points upward to the right. The left wrist and forearm form a straight line with the stick so that the left elbow is well out from the body. The stick is held at a 45° angle to the ground. The ball is about 2 feet from your feet, so you can move freely without overrunning the ball and increase the range of your vision.

Straight dribbling is used in an open field where the ball can be moved forward with a series of taps. The ball should be slightly outside your right foot. The force with which you hit the ball will depend on how much open space is available. Never hit the ball into a position where it is equally or more available to an opponent than to you!

Zigzag dribbling is done in preparation to go by (or beat) an opponent. You should alternately touch the ball with a

Dribble position.

Note the form of the player who is straight dribbling. You must always control your dribbling so that an opponent cannot intercept the ball.

forehand tap and a reverse stick tap, about 5 to 6 yards from your opponent. This technique will cause the ball to move in a zigzag fashion out in front of you. You should not, however, allow the ball to roll outside of either foot. To maneuver your stick over the ball, your left hand turns the stick through your slack right hand. The thumb of your right hand should be visible on the "up" side of the stick for both the forehand and reverse stick taps. Nonrhythmical tapping of the ball, faking a touch on the ball, changes of pace, body faking, and balance may all be combined in varying degrees to get you past your opponent. Remember, the important point is to leave your opponent behind you. In this critical aspect of field hockey, the player should be constantly reminded that the objective is to move the ball and herself past the opponent.

Forehand on zigzag dribble.

This player is exhibiting the most common faults in dribbling.

The left hand turns the stick through loose right hand to reverse stick tap on zigzag dribble.

Common Faults in Dribbling:

1. Ball too close to the feet.
2. Left wrist is bent.
3. Not lifting your head at times to see where you and the ball are going.
4. Back of your right hand is visible when doing the zigzag dribble.
5. The back of your left hand faces the path of the dribble, instead of facing upward and to the right.
6. The angle of the stick to the ground is too vertical, especially when dribbling to the right.

DRIBBLING TACTICS

Passing is the technique most often used to get behind defenders and into scoring position. At the right moment, however, a player (particularly a forward) should be able to beat a defender on her own. To do this she must upset her opponent's balance by using body and stick fakes. Then she accelerates past her opponent, while maintaining control of the ball. To confuse a defender, the attacker must move her body in combination with a zigzag ball movement and/or quick moves of the stick over the ball, but not touching it. Success depends on the variety and unpredictability of your moves. Effectiveness increases when your fakes are convincing. No fake is more useful than to fake a pass. This fake is executed in two stages. First, your body, eyes, and stick clearly indicate a pass and its direction. Then, at the last minute, when the defender reacts in the direction she thinks

the ball is going, you suddenly run in another direction. As soon as you are one full step past the defender you must cut in front of her, to make it difficult for her to tackle you. A pass following this move is often successful, because another defender must be drawn toward you (since you are a free and dangerous attacker), leaving one of your teammates free. For maximum effectiveness, these dribbling tactics should be confined to the attacking third of the field.

Passing dominates the midfield area. However, when you have lots of space and there is no one to pass to, it is wise to dribble forward or diagonally across the field with your eyes up, looking around the field for one of your teammates. Teammates take this as a cue to make

Dribbler cuts in front of beaten defender, making a tackle impossible. *Photo by Laurie Usher.*

Dribbler versus tackler is a typical 1 on 1 in game play. *Photo by Laurie Usher.*

moves that will free them to receive the ball. If a forward gets clear of all defenders, she might go straight to the goal. She must tap the ball farther ahead than normal, so that greater speed can be generated in avoiding the pursuit of the defenders. It is important to constantly practice these tactics aggressively, before they are tried out on your opponents in an actual game.

TACKLING TECHNIQUES

Of the 4 groups of techniques tackling is the only defensive technique, because the player does not have the ball when tackling. Tackling is the individual player's technique used to take the ball away from an opponent. It would be great not only to take the ball away from your opponent but also to gain possession of the ball every time; this is simply not possible and should not be expected. Good tackles often mean getting the ball out of the opponent's control and out of trouble. Sometimes a good tackle forces the ball away from an opponent, and onto the stick of an alert teammate.

The basic preparatory stance is very similar to that in many other sports. Your feet should be about shoulder width apart, one foot slightly in front of the other, with your weight evenly distributed. Bend your knees slightly (to give

Defender in basic stance ready to take on an approaching dribbler.

you a lower center of gravity), so that you can move quickly. Grip the stick (with your right hand slightly below the position used in dribbling) and hold it across your thighs, parallel to the ground, with the toe of the stick protruding beyond your body to the right. Keep your eyes on the ball. You may not physically interfere with the dribbler (your opponent), but if she loses control of the ball, release your stick from your right hand and poke the ball away from, preferably behind, the dribbler. The tackle is an explosive thrust or lunge of your stick onto the ball. Execute the tackle by using your left arm, left shoulder, and left foot to move your stick forward until you are fully extended. To keep your balance, your right shoulder and right arm should turn back and away from the direction of the tackle.

Front tackles are not always possible because the dribbler may keep control of the ball. If a front tackle is made and the ball is missed, you will be off balance and in no position to tackle again. The dribbler will then gain her objective of getting past you. When the dribbler is 3 to 6 yards away from you (depending on the dribbler's speed) and in control of the ball, you must be in position to make repeated tackles. You can only do this if you are running in the same direction, stride for stride, with the dribbler. This is referred to as tackling in retreat, because you are giving up ground in the direction of the goal you are defending. This is sound play, however, because you have not been beaten and left behind. If you see that you will have to retreat and tackle, take the basic stance but slightly overplay it to the left or right to force the dribbler in one direction or the other.

Tackling an Opponent on the Left

The tackler opens up by stepping toward her own goal line with her right foot, which pulls her right shoulder in the same direction. She is now in position to bring

Tackling on left while retreating. *Photo by Laurie Usher.*

her left foot around and run with the dribbler, keeping her hips level with and about a foot or 2 from the ball carrier's hips. While running, she keeps her eyes on the ball, waiting for it to rebound off the dribbler's stick. If she misses, she keeps running while gaining control of her stick and preparing to tackle again. On contact, the ball can be trapped under the tackler's stick as the dribbler overruns it, or pulled in toward the tackler, or poked to the left side of the dribbler. In all 3 of these cases the tackler should gain possession of the ball. The actual lunging for the ball from the left is very similar to the front tackle.

Tackling an Opponent on the Right

The tackler opens up in the same way as in the previous tackle, except that the first step is with the left foot. This tackle is done with the reverse stick, with everything else remaining the same. Reaching for the ball with the left foot, arm, and shoulder, the relationship of the tackler's hips to the ball carrier's hips, and the methods of winning the ball are the same as tackling on the left.

Tackling on right with 2 hands. *Photo by Mike Cash.*

Common Faults in Tackling:

1. Failing to watch the ball carefully.
2. Center of gravity too high, preventing or causing clumsy reach.
3. Failing to turn soon enough when tackling in retreat—opponent gets too close.
4. The first step on tackling in retreat is toward the sideline, not the goal line.
5. Using the right hand on the body of the dribbler when reverse stick tackling.
6. Not strong enough on the tackle, allowing the ball carrier to dribble through the tackler's stick.
7. Getting ahead of or overrunning the ball carrier, allowing her to reverse stick behind the tackler.
8. Tackler too far behind dribbler so that dribbler can cut in front of tackler.

TACKLING TACTICS

The most important aspect of tackling is the self-discipline necessary to refrain from charging or rushing at an opponent in possession of the ball. Except in the striking circle, a defender must not commit herself to a ball that is closer to an opponent. A defender who does so may look spectacular when she gets the ball but, like a basketball defender who constantly jumps in the air, she will be a detriment to her team against skilled opponents.

The dribbler attempts a series of body and stick fakes to confuse the defender. The tackler neutralizes the faking by concentrating on the ball only. By overplaying to one side of the oncoming dribbler, the defender can block the dribbler's freedom of movement and force her to go in one direction. Her reasons for doing this

Defender blocks dribbler's movement on the left, forcing her to go to the right, while running with her stride for stride.

may be to force the attacker in a direction away from her strength, to force the attacker toward the defender's strength, or to force the attacker in the direction of the defender's teammates (who can then double-team the attacker). If the defender is in a good position, she may cause the attacker to lose control of the ball by merely faking a move at the ball with her stick.

Dribbling and tackling should be taught together, so that maximum improvement can be made by both the attacker and defender.

RECEIVING TECHNIQUES

Fielding a ball that is either a pass from a teammate, a free ball, or an interception of the other team's pass is called receiving. Players must be able to receive balls at varying speeds, with difficult bounces, and from many angles, while running, and often when being challenged by an opponent. A well-received ball is completely controlled by the player, so that a second touch such as a hit, pass, or dribble is immediately possible. A ball that deflects away from the receiver or up in the air forces the receiver to chase the ball or wait for the ball. That lost time gives your opponent time to get to the ball. A ball that is hit into a mattress won't rebound because the mattress "gives." But a ball hit against a cinder block wall will rebound greatly because there is no give. The receiver of a hockey ball must give like a mattress in order to absorb the speed of the ball and cushion it. The tension of your grip, particularly your right hand, must be adjusted to develop a "soft" stick that can immediately cushion a hard hit. In receiving, as in dribbling, a very sound rule is to never allow the ball to be equally available or more available to your opponent than it is to you.

Because you must receive balls from

Because stick is not inclined forward ball is aerially deflected, preventing an immediate, accurate second touch.

many directions, your grip will change and the point of receiving in relation to your feet will differ. There are several things, however, that are constant regardless of the angle or direction of the ball. You must focus your eyes and mind on the ball at the moment it touches your stick. The blade of your stick must be at a right angle to the direction from which the ball is coming, to avoid deflection. Also, the ball must be trapped to avoid

Ball trapped on hook of stick.

rebounds into the air. To trap the ball, incline the blade of your stick toward the ground to form a wedge-shaped area. The ball will be trapped and forced to the ground. Receiving, particularly trapping, is much more effective when you allow the ball to come to your stick, rather than moving your stick to meet the ball. Your body must be balanced, but your center of gravity should not be so low that swift movement is awkward.

Receiving a ball coming toward you: The grip for receiving is like that for dribbling. The stick should be angled across the front of your body, which should be lined up behind the ball so that the head of the stick is inside your right foot. Your left hand will be thigh height, just left of your left thigh. Your left wrist and forearm should be a straight extension of the stick.

Receiving a ball coming from your left: You should grip the stick with your hands a little farther apart than in the dribbling grip. Let the ball cross your left leg and take it just inside your right foot. Your feet and body should be clearly behind the ball. Your left shoulder should face the direction from which the ball is coming. The stick must be comfortably in front of the body to form coordinated and continuous movement.

Receiving a ball coming from your right: Use the same grip as above. With the ball not too far ahead of you, keep your feet moving toward the goal, but twist your torso so that you face the direction from which the ball is coming. Your shoulders should be at right angles to the goal lines. Angle the stick across your body, with your left wrist and forearm forming a straight extension of the stick. Take the ball in midstride.

When a ball is coming from your right, but is so far ahead that it cannot be taken in midstride, take it with a reverse stick. With the toe of the stick on the ground,

Player has just received a pass from her left.

Player has just received a pass from her right with reverse stick.

Player receives a pass from her right in midstride. *Photo by Laurie Usher.*

your left hand grips the stick from the left with the back of your left hand facing the opposite direction from which the ball is coming. Your right hand takes the stick from the right, below the left hand, with the back of the right hand facing the ball. Your right shoulder should face the direction from which the ball is coming. Take the ball on the toe of your stick, in front of and between your feet.

Receiving a ball coming from behind you on the left: This is basically the same as receiving the ball coming from the left. To avoid obstruction, however, your feet must face your opponents' goal, which means you have to look over your left shoulder to see the approaching ball. It is very important to allow the ball to cross your body, so it can be taken in front of your feet.

Receiving a ball coming from behind you on the right: Unless the pass is coming to you at a very slight angle, you must take the ball with a reverse stick. The technique is the same as the reverse stick on fielding a ball from the right, except

your feet must face your opponents' goal to avoid obstruction. You must watch the ball by looking over your right shoulder. Again, allow the ball to cross your body so that you can take it in front of your feet.

Receiving an aerial ball: Although an aerial ball can be fielded with your hand,

Fielding an aerial ball.

it is advisable to use your stick, because the rule allowing you to use your hand is so limiting. By using your stick the ball can be guided down to the ground in any direction. The most important point is to incline your stick forward in order to direct the ball to the ground. Striking an aerial ball, or hitting it on the fly, is potentially very dangerous and must be penalized. The grip and position of the hands is the same as in the dribble, but the hands are farther apart. Your left elbow is very high, with your right elbow pointing back if the ball is on your right, or pointing right if the ball is on your left. By inclining your stick forward you are really trapping the ball in the air thereby forcing it to the ground in a playable position.

Common Faults in Receiving:

1. Turning the blade of your stick away from the direction of the ball, causing a deflection.
2. Inclining your stick backward, causing an upward deflection of the ball.

The ball is coming from this player's left. Because the blade is angled away from the direction of the ball, the ball will be deflected forward and to the player's right.

3. Failing to allow the ball to come to your stick, particularly when running to meet it.
4. Failing to concentrate on the ball at the moment of contact with your stick.
5. Turning your feet to face a pass coming from the rear, thereby setting up a possible obstruction.

STRIKING TECHNIQUES

Hit

The hit is a technique needed to pass a long distance, or to shoot at the goal. There is a premium on power as well as accuracy. You will have to hit from a stationary position, or on the move following a dribble, or immediately after receiving the ball. The hit can be broken down into 5 parts. It is important, however, that the backswing, downswing, ball contact, and follow-through be one fluid motion with no break in action.

Grip: With the stick held in the position shown in this photo, your left hand is placed on the stick with the back of your hand facing the direction of the intended hit. Your right hand should be placed on the stick from the right side, directly below and touching your left forefinger. To bring your hands together for a hit when you are playing, it is preferable for your right hand to slide up to your left hand. Your left hand can slide down to your right hand, which makes for a quicker hit, but with less power.

Stance: Your feet should be shoulder width apart, with your right foot facing the direction of your torso, and your left foot about 40° more toward the other team's goal line. Your left shoulder faces the intended direction of the hit. The ball is opposite the heel of your left foot and must not be out so far that you lose your

The grip and stance for the hit.

muscles must be tense. Your arms and stick must be straight at the bottom of the swing. Keep your eyes on the ball and follow straight through with the stick in the direction of the hit. Your wrists must control the stick in order to stop the stick at waist level.

Power: Power in hitting the ball comes from your body's momentum (or approach speed), the proper shift of your weight, your upper-body strength, and acceleration of the downswing (so that the stick has reached maximum speed at impact). Your left leg and left side must be strong not only to give you a powerful swing but also to maintain stability in your swing.

balance reaching for it, and not so close that your arms are cramped. The ball must be positioned in such a way that the stick can be swung freely.

Backswing: Move the stick back in a straight line, without letting your arms touch any part of your body, until your wrists are just below waist level. Your left arm should be straight, and your right elbow should be 6 to 8 inches from your ribs. Cock your wrists so that the head of the stick is slightly above your right hand and the toe of the stick points upward. Your wrists and grip must remain firm. Shift your weight to your right foot.

Downswing, Ball Contact, and Follow-through: Just prior to the downswing shift your weight to your left leg. You will get a hard hit by accelerating the speed of your stick in a straight line toward the ball. At the moment you hit the ball, all of your shoulder, arm, wrist, and hand

The follow-through after the hit. *Photo by Laurie Usher.*

Common Faults in Hitting:

1. Improper positioning of the ball.
2. Topping the ball, caused by taking your eyes off it.

3. Not swinging in a straight line.
4. Hitting at the ball and not through it.
5. Slowing the stick at contact.
6. Elbows tucked in and contacting the body.
7. The right elbow jutting well out from the body so that the upper arm is level with the shoulder.
8. Feet too close, causing loss of balance—or too far apart, causing a slow reaction to the next move.
9. Executing too slowly or executing in sections—making a backswing and then running several yards before making the downswing.
10. Lack of muscular tension during downswing and at impact.

Hitting to the Left: This is easier if the ball is off the left foot. Either move the ball there with your stick or move your body to the right of the ball.

Hitting to the Right: To hit the ball in this direction you must move your feet and twist your torso so that your right shoulder is pulled back, as the left shoulder turns toward the target. Or, you can pull the ball back with a reverse stick, as your body pivots (bringing your left side into proper position).

Push

The push is used to pass over short distances. Pushes are invaluable because they can be executed quickly without much preliminary action. Great control of speed and accuracy can be given to the ball, and a push can be performed off a dribble or after receiving the ball.

The grip for the push is similar to the grip for dribbling, but your right hand should be a little farther below your left hand on the shaft of the stick. Your body must be sideways to the line of the pass, with your left shoulder pointing in the

Player has just pushed the ball.

direction of the pass. Your center of gravity must be lowered. Your feet should be slightly more than shoulder width apart, with the toes of both feet pointing in the same direction as the hit. Your left wrist and forearm should be a straight extension of the stick, with your left elbow well out from your body. Incline your stick at a 35° to 45° angle from the ground. The ball should be off the heel of your left foot and directly under your eyes. There is no backswing in the push, so the stick must be placed directly behind the ball.

Execute the push by having your right hand and wrist forcefully push the stick through the ball in opposition to your left hand and wrist (which exert pressure in a backward direction). This movement must be fast, and must be assisted with a strong shifting of weight from your right foot to your left foot. Follow through by continuing to move the head of the stick in the direction of the pass. Be sure to extend your right leg on the follow-through.

Common Faults in the Push:

1. Facing the direction of intended push

instead of getting your left shoulder around.

2. Keeping your center of gravity too high, with your body too upright.
3. Poor coordination of weight shifting.
4. Right foot forward.
5. Failure to have your left hand and wrist forward prior to the actual release of the push.
6. Keeping the stick too vertical.
7. Unnecessary motions with the stick behind the ball just before the push.

Flick

The flick is a lofted ball that is a valuable though infrequently used technique for passing through defenders or over their sticks. Its greatest value, however, is in shooting for a goal, because the area of the goal highest off the ground can be utilized in beating the goalkeeper.

Flicking is very similar to pushing. One of the differences is that the ball placement is farther forward in the flick. The underside of the blade is under the ball, so that the blade is angled up and the handle is inclined back from the hook toward you. Begin the action with your weight shifting onto your bent right leg. Combine this quick shift of your body forward with a forceful movement of your right forearm, and a strong wrist action, in the direction of the pass. Like the push, the follow-through is a continuation in the direction of the pass.

The follow-through after the flick. *Photo by Laurie Usher.*

The flick.

Common Faults in the Flick:

1. Same kind of faults as in the push.
2. Poor wrist movement at the moment of action.
3. Ball not far enough forward, or too far forward.
4. Not positioning your body back far enough or low enough to get under the ball.

It takes a lot of practice to develop the skill Chris Larson exhibits as she flicks the ball past her opponent. *Photo by Laurie Usher.*

Chapter 6
TRAINING AND PRACTICE

Before players can play field hockey intelligently, they must be technically sound and well-schooled in basic individual, group, and team tactics. These are all interrelated and overlapping. Proficiency in field hockey results from successful execution of techniques and tactics. How many goals have not been scored because the shooter lacked technique, or decided on the wrong technique, or used superb technique only to hit the goalkeeper squarely on the pads? Results count. If it works, it is right! Coaches should accept the style of some players, even though it may be unorthodox, if that style does not interfere with the concept of team play. Coaches and experienced players, however, must recognize that beginning players may not be aware of their own mistakes. They may not even be able to take advantage of each other's mistakes. A clear example of this is a forward who does not immediately recognize her advantage when she has beaten a defender who blindly charged at the ball.

Preseason practice and hockey camp are the places to thoroughly learn the theory and objectives of basic techniques and tactics and how they apply to the game. Explanations must be clear and concise so that their application is of practical value. When players understand the logic of what they are doing they are much more willing and enthusiastic about the necessity of repetition that is needed for proper execution. Watching a coach or another player (whether in a game or on film) execute a technique or tactic properly is a very effective way to learn field hockey.

TECHNIQUES FOR TRAINING

There are 4 steps in successful field hockey training:

1. Fundamental positioning of body parts, stick, and ball. This technique is carried out in slow motion with reduced power and strength, but with full concentration.

2. When your form is good (which it will be in a very short time) gradually add running to your training. Start slowly and build up speed as your efficiency improves. Ball control with speed will be the result. A player who moves with the ball under control at 80% of her running speed is consistently more valuable to her team than a player who is always at top speed but cannot control the ball.

3. Next, add passive pressure to your training by working with an opponent who will execute her game movements in slow motion so that you can clearly see the challenge you face.

4. Finally, advance to active pressure, which means practicing under game-like conditions. Most technique practices are with active pressure, because that is the way the game is played. Return to one of the previous training steps only if you pinpoint a persistent problem. Then you can slowly analyze and solve the problem.

TECHNIQUES FOR PRACTICING

Practice is designed to help you develop a feeling for the ball and to help you coordinate your body and stick movements. At first you should work at 50% speed and power. Full concentration is a must. At the beginning of the season, and sporadically throughout the season, it is very wise to practice your techniques in a gym or parking lot (if the field is not a particularly good one). This forces you to execute the field hockey techniques properly. When you are playing on a field you must expect bad bounces, make some adjustments, and accept some misses—but the basic techniques are the same. Practicing properly and repeatedly makes for perfect playing!

Dribbling and Faking

1. Pull the ball left and right alternately using the forehand and reverse stick. Don't let the ball move outside either foot. The stick should be moved quickly to wait for the ball after each tap. Shift your weight from one leg to the other. How many taps in 30 seconds?

2. Tap the ball in a series to the left and then to the right. You must move your feet fast enough to beat the ball. Changes of direction must be sharp. Look up. Play follow the leader.

3. Tap the ball to your left only, but between each tap bring the stick over the ball as in a reverse stick tap, but don't touch it. Bring the stick back and tap it with your forehand. The ball is only touched on the forehand and faked on the reverse stick. Reverse the procedure to your right. Look up.

4. Combine #2 and #3 in a random fashion. Look up. Shift your weight to the side of the fake. Play follow the leader.

5. Run a straight line, but zigzag the ball diagonally across the line. Look up.

6. Run a straight line. Move the ball in a straight line. Don't tap the ball often, but between taps move the stick back and forth over the ball. Look up.

7. Creative dribbling: Move in a random manner. Dribble around using everything from the preceding exercises. Look up. Fake. Change rhythm. Change speed. Suddenly change your direction. Your feet must keep up with the ball. Keep maximum contact of your stick on the ball, or keep the stick moving quickly over the ball.

8. Do #7 in the striking circle, with 7 to

10 other players doing the same thing. Avoid each other by doing all things done previously. Fake convincingly. Look up. Read the direction and speed of others. Read the direction of the weight shift of others. Be ready, in close quarters, to move past more than one other player. Maintain maximum contact on the ball or stick activity over the ball. After a fake move as quickly as a cat.

9. Exercises #7 and #8 can be done starting with 30 seconds and building to 3 minutes. In between, practice aerial tapping. How many consecutive aerial taps can you do in 30 seconds? Tap 5 times and then do a full turn and keep tapping. Aerial tap with a partner. Use your imagination.

10. Tag games can be adapted for dribbling, faking, and beating an opponent. Each player is given a ball. Tagging can be done with one of your hands, a gentle tap with the stick (on hips or buttocks), or by tapping your opponent's ball away.

Players who practice on their own will most effectively and cleverly maneuver the stick and ball. Players who practice only when the coach is there (during organized practice) may be adequate, but they will not be the players who improvise, and who win games by suddenly changing the tempo and pattern of play.

Passing Alone

1. Make a target using cones, or tape a target on the base of a wall. Hit or push the ball accurately. Decrease the size of the target and/or increase your distance from the target.

2. Do #1 as a dribble. Change the angle of your dribble to the target.

3. Set out a cone that represents an op-

ponent and do #1 after beating your "opponent." Vary the side and method of passing by the cone.

4. Practice "give and go" with a wall. Pass the ball to the wall and move quickly. If you judged the angles correctly, the ball will rebound back to you without your breaking your stride. Continue passing along the length of the wall.

Passing in Combination

Haphazard passing to the receiver is one of the most common errors in field hockey. During practice, I impose a light punishment on sloppy passers. My apologies to the psychologists, but this is one area where I feel justified in punishing players for a sloppy technique. I do it pleasantly and the logic of the punishment is not denied by the players. Any ball that impels a receiver to stop or chase was not properly passed. Therefore, the passer has to retrieve the ball. A good pass is one where the receiver takes the ball, while she is still moving and without breaking her stride.

A good pass!

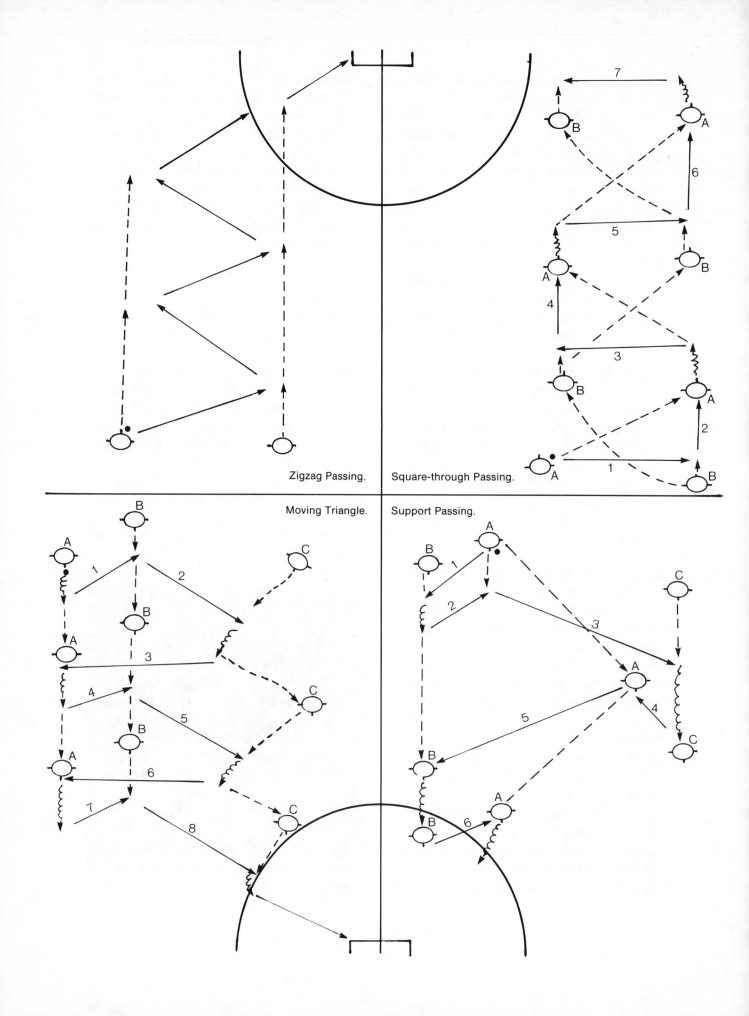

Zigzag Passing.

Square-through Passing.

Moving Triangle.

Support Passing.

Finish the following passing sequences by taking a shot at the goal.

1. Zigzag passing. Players run parallel to each other. The ball moves zigzag down the field.
2. Square-through passing. When receiving a "square" pass, with the ball moving parallel to the goal line, the receiver must be running up from behind (and to the side of) the passer to take the ball. A "through" pass moves the ball parallel to the sideline, with the receiver running diagonally into open space to take the ball. In this sequence player A passes square to player B. Player A immediately sprints diagonally for a through pass from B. B immediately sprints diagonally to receive a square pass. A always passes square, but receives through passes. B always passes through, but receives square passes.
3. Moving triangle. This pattern features diagonal, square, and back passing. Player A on the right starts with the ball. Player B is behind A in a support position. Player C is wide to the left of and level with player A. This triangle is not equal-sided. Player A dribbles a little and passes back to B. As B receives the ball C moves diagonally and receives a diagonal pass from B. Player A moves forward, but remains slightly behind player C, to receive a square pass from C. C re-establishes her distance to the left of A as A passes back to B. The series keeps repeating itself (about 3 times), while moving down the field.
4. Support passing. Player A, the support player, passes to player B. B passes back to A. A then passes to player C. A runs over to receive a support pass from C. A passes to B and runs over to support her.

Receiving Alone

To do this you bounce the ball off a wall with no baseboard, so that the ball will bounce smoothly off the wall and back to you.

1. Get your body into the proper position to receive the ball from the "passer" (in this case from the wall). Allow yourself enough distance from the wall to have time to get into the proper position to receive the ball after you hit it.
2. Repeat exercise four, under Passing Alone.

PRACTICING TACTICS

In any game of field hockey you will be attacking or defending at different points in the game. Therefore, it is necessary for you to practice attack and defense by having some of your teammates on your side and some of your teammates acting as your opponents. During practice, teammates on opposite sides must compete just as fiercely as they would against opponents in an actual game. Only when you and your teammates are willing to compete this intensely in practice will your team consistently succeed in games.

Players like and dislike teammates off the field. But in practice, as in games, personalities don't matter. Cooperation and competition are both essential for good practice sessions. Players must work and make decisions according to the tactical situations they face—*not* according to personal relationships and feelings among teammates in off-field social situations. What happens in practice, happens in a game.

Individual Tactics

When you are dribbling, about to pass or receive, you will be challenged by an opponent. Your team will gain or lose ball possession as the result of such a duel. If

1 on 1 during 1976 collegiate championship game. *Photo by Laurie Usher.*

you win this duel then your team wins the ball and can attack, score, and win the game. This fact should make clear the necessity for you to frequently and aggressively practice 1 on 1 situations. The value of 1 on 1 practice is that it allows you to perfect every tactic required to maintain or gain ball possession. The total outcome of the successful 1 on 1 duels in a game usually decides the victor. No matter what tactics you use, you must know the rules because on every foul the ball is gained or lost.

1. 1 on 1—dribbling and tackling. A keep-away game with no goals in which the player with the ball keeps it away from her opponent. When possession changes, roles change. On the transition (change of possession) there is no break—players must go from one job to the other without rest. Practice this exercise 1 to 3 minutes.

2. Same as #1 with makeshift goals. Every time you score you keep possession. The principle of counterattacking is crucial in this situation. When the tackler clearly wins the ball she should break for the goal with no hesitation. Practice this exercise 1 to 3 minutes.

3. Same as #2 with 1 or 2 regulation goals and a goalkeeper.

Group Tactics

Principles of team play and other important factors become a definite part of group tactics. When practicing group tactics, do not focus on any 1 player or any single aspect of play. Simply criticizing a player because she never gets the ball does not tell you or her why she never gets the ball. The problem may be due to a combination of factors: the speed, timing, or accuracy of the pass; poor techniques; the receiver may not move quickly enough or may move into the wrong space; the receiver may not fake before she tries to receive a pass; or a pass may not be feasible because the defender is doing such a good job.

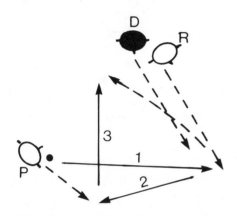

2 on 1. Play should be continuous. All moves should be timed according to the actions of the defender.

1. 2 on 1—Two attackers pass the ball to each other by having the player without the ball run into open space to receive the pass. Mobility is very important. The defender pressures the player without the ball and tries to intercept the pass.

2. 2 on 1—This exercise is primarily designed for practicing give-and-go passing (with one attacker giving the ball to her partner and running behind the defender to receive her partner's pass). The defender is unrestricted as to whom she marks or pressures and should fake moves at the attacker with the ball to upset her timing. the attacker with the ball should, at times, fake the pass and dribble past the defender. This prevents the defender from always assuming that an attacker will pass to her partner.

3. 1 on 1 plus a neutral player—The neutral player always practices give-and-go passing with whichever player is in possession of the ball. There are always 2 attackers and 1 defender. This is good practice for midfield players. Quick transition from attack to defense is important. The neutral player cannot score. Mobility is crucial.

You can be flexible in your method of ending the previous 3 games: you may not permit any goal scoring; you may use

2 on 1 practice of group tactics.

small, makeshift goals; you may use regulation goals with a goalkeeper; or a combination of the last 2.

4. 3 on 1 with no goals. Begin with the players in the middle in possession and the other 2 on either side of them. Pass directly and move. The third player without the ball (on the team of 3 players) moves in relation to her teammates. The player with the ball always has a teammate on either side. Don't always ball-watch. The defender always takes the ball. If she touches it or wins it she replaces the player at fault, who then becomes the defender.

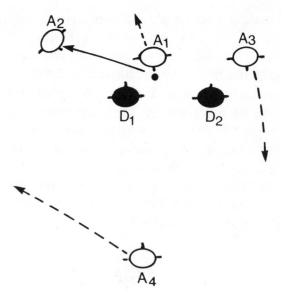

4 on 2. The player with the ball must always be supported by a teammate on each side of her and a fourth team member free to receive a through ball. Defenders must prevent through passes. As the play continues the roles will change.

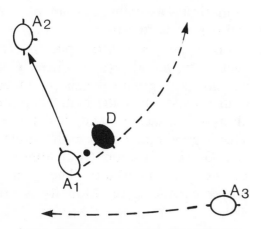

3 on 1. The two players without the ball travel the shortest and simplest route. They should not both cross behind the defender at the same time.

5. 4 on 2 with no goals. The player with the ball must always be supported by 2 teammates, one on either side of her. The fourth player moves to a position where she can get a through pass. As the ball moves these roles constantly change. The player who has the ball should, at times, fake a pass one way and go the other. Look up. Once the players get the feel of this action, start passing and moving. This forces the 2 teammates to look and move so that the player with the ball always has support on either side. Of course, the

through pass. The defenders try to win the ball with an interception tackle. This is a superb drill for defenders because one defender must pressure the ball and the other must cover to prevent a through pass. Count the passes. Count the through passes. The defender changes teams with the player at fault for losing possession. Who never becomes a defender?

6. 4 on 4 with goals—Practice give-and-go passing, dribbling and faking, support and back passing, man-to-man marking, and counterattacking.

Team Tactics

Team tactics are designed to coordinate the team's defensive structure, improve offensive cooperation, speed up the transition from defense to offense (or vice versa), and/or practice special plans for a particular opponent.

1. 6 on 6 on half the field—The offense, forwards, and midfielders play against

the goalkeeper and the defense (to make the techniques and group tactics work within the big game). The attackers try for a good shot at the goal or at least a penalty corner. The defenders must prevent the attackers from scoring or being awarded a penalty corner. After taking the ball away from the attackers, the defenders interpass the ball to midfield. When the attacking forward loses possession of the ball, she must immediately work to get the ball back while her teammates retreat almost to midfield. This transition must be done spontaneously with no break in team play.

2. 8 on 8 on a full field—Each team has 3 forwards, 1 midfielder, 3 defenders, and 1 goalkeeper. Many of the reasons for doing #1 apply to this exercise, except that the whole field is used in this case. This exercise is particularly valuable for practicing the setting-up passing in midfield.

3. 11 on 11—The high school or college coach must decide whether the varsity should play against the junior varsity squad, or whether the varsity squad should be divided into two teams of attackers and defenders.

The goalkeeper's job has unique requirements. She must have great agility to make quick stops and quick changes of direction. *Photo by Laurie Usher.*

Chapter 7
GOALKEEPING

The goalkeeper is her team's last line of defense. She must try to prevent the other team from scoring a goal by stopping shots with her legs, stick, or hands. That accomplished, she must be able to clear the ball with her feet or stick. The goalkeeper must accept, even relish, this challenge of keeping goal. She has unique requirements and needs regular practice to do her job properly. At first, the coach should allow the goalkeeper to simply act on her own instincts in keeping the ball out of the goal. Coaches must have open minds on new ideas and equipment. They must find the right balance between results and techniques. If a novice goalkeeper uses unorthodox techniques that work and won't interfere with her future developments, that's fine. However, unorthodox goalkeeping should not contradict such basic goalkeeping principles as lining up the ball, playing correct angles, and maintaining a balanced, comfortable, and stable stance.

PHYSICAL QUALIFICATIONS

1. Speed of reaction and movement.
2. Agility—quick stops, quick changes of direction, and great speed in getting up off the ground.
3. Basic flexibility to stop a ball while she is fully extended.

PSYCHOLOGICAL QUALIFICATIONS

1. Courage—indispensable regardless of physical qualities. The goalkeeper will not succeed if every shot at the goal frightens her.
2. Concentration—the goalkeeper must watch the ball and the patterns of play during an entire game. One lapse in concentration during a game can mean losing the game.
3. Confidence—the keeper must be certain within herself that she can do the job. This takes time and the coach and keeper must be patient. Confidence eliminates inconsistencies in the goalkeeper's performance. Confidence can

change from game to game or even within a game. Usually a good save early in a game is all the keeper needs. Working hard and giving her maximum effort help a keeper gain confidence in herself, and her confidence affects her teammates. She must not show nervousness, or feel the need to always apologize for her mistakes.

4. Anticipation—the ability to predict what will happen next, to react a split second before the ball arrives. This ability comes from experience and knowledge of the goalkeeper's position *and* the whereabouts of potential scorers. You should never offer your teammates the lame excuse, "I didn't see her!"

BASIC STANCE

All moves are made from this basic, ready-to-act position. The keeper must essentially be balanced, controlled, and poised for quick and easy movement. She must be in her stance the whole time the ball is active in the defending third of the field, and sooner if a breakaway is possible. However, her concentration must not waver when she is out of her stance. Follow these instructions for creating the basic stance:

1. Keep your feet shoulder width apart.
2. Keep your legs comfortably bent.
3. Keep your body weight evenly distributed on the balls of your feet.
4. Incline your body slightly forward.
5. Keep your forearms parallel to the ground.
6. Hold your stick in your glove hand open, facing out, and slightly ahead of your body.
7. Hold your stick in your right hand as high as possible and pointing slightly in front of the right goalpost.

8. Keep your eyes on the ball. Most of the game the goalkeeper watches the travels of the ball.

Common Faults in Basic Stance:

1. Standing with feet too close, preventing good balance and quick movement.
2. Standing with feet too far apart, preventing lateral movement.
3. Standing with weight too far forward or backward. The latter situation is often the result of a lack of physical courage.
4. Coming unglued—losing the compactness of the stance when moving.
5. Taking steps that are too large when moving to prevent a goal.

PRINCIPLES OF GOALKEEPING

There are 3 very important principles of correct goalkeeping. Against accurate, clever shooters you cannot violate these principles and successfully defend your goal.

1. Narrowing the angle—This means taking away some of the attacker's shooting space by coming off the goal line. Timidity (not coming far enough out from the goal line) and recklessness (coming off the goal line too soon and/or too far) will both result in a goal being scored against your team.
2. Remaining stationary when your opponent is in a scoring position—Charging out at an attacker in control of the ball can be spectacular but very unreliable. You must move early so you are ready, with the shooting angle narrowed, so that when the attacker shoots you can react in any direction.
3. Lining up with the ball—You must position yourself on an imaginary line

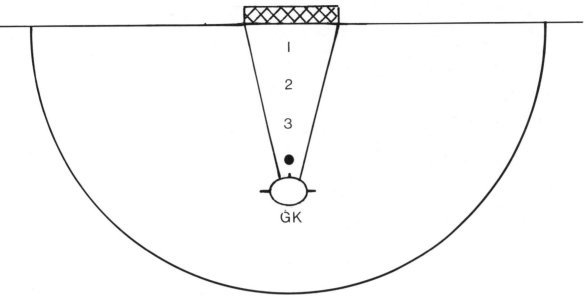

Narrowing the Angle. Clearly the goalkeeper reduces the shooter's chance for a goal by taking position 3.

between your body and the ball, not the attacker. One exception to this rule is when you know something about the shooter and/or you want to influence the direction of the shot.

SAVES

Kicking ability means nothing if the goalkeeper cannot stop a shot. The first priority must be saving the goal.

Saves with Your Legs

Basically, you want to stop the ball on your pads in such a way that you control the rebound. Your legs must be together and inclined forward, similar to the angle of a field player's stick when she receives the ball. If you have enough time, a slight rebound can be helpful because you can take a short step with your nonkicking leg (giving you more power) before clearing

Goalkeeper narrows angle in front of goal during indoor game.

Goalkeeper saves with legs together and inclined forward to control rebound and prepare for her next move.

the ball from the goal area. How much rebound you allow depends on how much time you have and how far away your nearest opponent is.

When you stop a ball with one of your legs fully extended you will hardly be able to control the rebound. In that case, you will have to use your stick to clear the ball from the goal area, since it would take too long for you to get up off the ground to kick the ball.

Saves with Your Hand

Stopping the ball with your hand is controversial. The rules do permit a slightly forward rebound from the goalkeeper's hand, but referees differ in their interpretations of such rebounds. To avoid this type of problem you should momentarily catch the ball, immediately drop it straight down with no rebound, and clear it with your foot. This way there can be no misinterpretation leading to a penalty stroke. One of the most difficult saves you will have to make is the flick to the upper left corner of the goal. You cannot reach it with your right leg, and using your stick above your shoulder will surely be whistled as a foul. You must reach

across your body and over your head with your left hand to stop the shot.

Saves with Your Stick

This type of save is used on a ground shot that you cannot reach with your right leg fully extended. It also is used for aerial shots on your right that are awkward or impossible for you to reach with your right leg or your left hand. You must control your stick, and not swing wildly at the ball, so as to avoid dangerous play.

CLEARING

After preventing a goal you must put the ball out of danger. You can use either an "instep clear" or a "toe clear." The latter requires an overboot with a reinforced, flat kicking surface. Your first priority is to kick the ball hard and far, but if time permits you should also try to be accurate. For emergencies you must be able to use your other foot, although the clear will not be as powerful.

Instep Clear

Your nonkicking leg must be stable beside the ball. Keep your eyes focused on the ball. As in the instep kick in soccer, your

Goalkeeper saves ground shot with her stick.

kicking foot should be brought back from your hip, with the knee bent. The ankle of your kicking leg must be firm and your toes should point down so that the ball is hit solidly with your instep. Kick through the ball and follow through as far as possible in the direction of the kick, with your toes pointed down to avoid a potentially dangerous aerial clear. The instep clear can be more accurate than the toe clear because of larger contact surface available on the instep.

Goalkeeper saves with the instep clear.

Toe Clear

The toe clear lacks the sophistication of the instep clear but that is its advantage. A primitive response under pressure is often to use your toe to clear the ball. When your equipment permits this, pain free, it adds to your efficiency. The placement of your nonkicking leg, the position of your head and eyes, the movement of your kicking leg, knee, and your follow-through are the same as for the instep clear. The difference is the contact point, in this case your toe.

Stick Clear

The stick is used in desperation when you are down or in a very awkward position and you cannot use your feet. If there is time you should grip the stick with both hands.

Clearing on the Fly

As a goalkeeper, if you see a loose ball or a through pass that you can reach before anyone else and the ball is inside the striking circle, go for it! Move quickly and aggressively, ignore the other team's forwards, and concentrate totally on the

Goalkeeper moves quickly and aggressively, clearing on the fly.

moving ball. The techniques previously described also apply to this kind of clear, except that the ball is moving.

LEADERSHIP

The goalkeeper has the final say. If you can clearly reach the ball before any of your teammates you must call out "mine" or "keeper" right away. Then make sure you take the ball! Your teammates must listen and respond to your commands. Your nearest teammate should cover for you by entering the goal the moment you move out to take the ball. You must specifically direct players in some situations: "Susie, pick up number 14."; "Ann, drop back and cover."; or "You have time, Maude." Idle and general chatter like "hurry," "mark, mark," or "attaway" are unnecessary, frantic, and display your ignorance of the tactical situation on the playing field.

PRACTICES AND DRILLS

Do not enter the goal until you are ready and warmed-up. Develop your own ritual—dress your left leg first, measure the goalmouth from left to right, step off the striking circle, smack each leg 3 times with your stick. You must be eager to practice, have a sense of humor, and a realistic attitude toward the game—after all, good players with enough time in scoring position should score. You should not expect to have someone paying attention to you all the time. You will have to work alone at times in and out of pads. You must work on skills you have trouble with, without totally neglecting the skills you have mastered. Coaches should not leave you on your own too long or force you into idleness, because coaches must reinforce the theme: "What you do in practice is what you do in the game!" As far as your teammates' behavior during practice is concerned, you should step out of the goal if shooters practice their shots in an unfair or unprofessional manner. And finally, goalkeepers and shooters must develop a sense of when to play with power and accuracy and when to play with finesse and accuracy.

Drills must be designed according to the specific aspect of the game for which you are training. Some of the drills are overlapping in their content, but the correct stance and basic principles of goalkeeping must be constantly emphasized. Drills are always performed with the goalkeeper dressed in full equipment.

Stance, Recovery, Balance, Agility

1. Every now and then the coach should unexpectedly give you a shove. Are you stable?
2. Lie on the ground in positions similar to those you might expect to assume in a game. Practice quickly recovering your basic stance. Your sequence of recovery should be to (a) find the ball, (b) get to your knee(s), and (c) resume your basic stance.
3. Stance course—Make an 8-yard square with cones. Perform different movements between the cones. Run between cones 1 and 2, carioca between cones 2 and 4, run backwards from cone 4 to cone 1, sidestep between cones 1 and 2, run between cones 2 and 3, etc. You must maintain your proper balance at all times.

Saves

1. Rapid-fire defense—Ten players, each with a ball, line up on the rim of the striking circle. One after the other they shoot at the goal. You must stop each shot from scoring. Each shot comes cuted after your previous save but before you are fully set to defend against it. Try some variations: number the players randomly so you don't know who is shooting next, or move the players closer to the goal and repeat the random shooting with pushes and flicks toward the goal.
2. Shooter A is in position at the edge of the striking circle. Shooter B is 6 yards opposite the right goalpost. Shooter A takes a shot at the goal and, as soon as you stop the ball, shooter B lightly tosses a ball into the air for you to execute an aerial save. You can practice several variations of these positions.

Clearing

The previous drills can be used, but this time you must clear the ball from the goal area each time you make a save.

Rebounds

Again, the same drills as before, but this time each shooter (alone or with another player) follows the rebounding ball after you clear it from the goal area.

Deflections

You must always be prepared to react quickly to a change in direction of a shot toward the goal. The ball may be intentionally deflected by another attacker or unintentionally deflected by a teammate and you must immediately change your position according to the movement of the ball. No matter who deflects the ball, if it crosses the goal line the attacking team will score!

1. The previous drills can be used again. This time, though, put a player 7 yards away from the goalmouth. Each shooter tries to score a goal as before. The player opposite the goal tries to touch the ball just enough to change its direction so that you have to line yourself up with the ball again. Repeat the drills, but move the deflecting player closer and closer to the goal.

Blind Drills

At times you will have to find the ball when your vision is temporarily blocked. Hopefully, this won't occur very often but you should be prepared.

1. For this drill, keep your back to the shooters. The shooters take turns in making shots at the goal but each shooter calls out "shot," as she shoots

In her defense against a penalty stroke, keeper's feet are slightly too wide for quick lateral movement. *Photo by Laurie Usher.*

toward the goal. Your job is to turn around, locate the ball, and try to prevent a goal from being scored—as soon as you hear the word "shot."

Positional Drills

These drills are designed to make you shift every time the ball moves. The one time you are careless is the one time you could be beaten.

1. About 7 yards in front of the goal 2 shooters, 9 yards apart, pass back and forth. You shift your position to follow the ball on every pass. A shot could come at any time. One of the passers should try a faked pass followed by a shot at the goal to test your concentration.
2. Have the 2 shooters pass back and forth as they gradually move toward the goal from the 25-yard line.

PENALTY STROKE

You should not feel badly when an official awards a penalty stroke to a member of the attacking team during a game, unless it was justified and you could have prevented it. For the goalkeeper, a penalty stroke is just one more opportunity to stop the other team from scoring. You must realize, however, that a powerful, accurate stroke placed just inside either goalpost cannot be saved unless you anticipate the direction of the ball correctly and make a dive to stop it. If you guess wrong, even a feebly hit ball (if placed on the opposite side of your dive) will roll into the goal. On a penalty stroke, I believe you should only try to stop "savable" shots. You might as well accept any shot that is just inside of either goalpost.

Don't maintain any eye contact with the stroker or the other team. Take your time, take a few deep breaths, and shake

know something about the stroker, try standing a little to one side to tempt the stroker to shoot for the wide side. If you know which side the shooter will try for, you have a very good chance to save a goal.

Hold your stick loosely with both hands, palms down. You must be prepared to quickly take one hand off the stick, if necessary, in order to stop an aerial shot with your hand. Hold your stick parallel to the ground about waist-high. Keep your eyes on the ball and maintain the correct basic stance. If you take your position on the goal line too early, you will be too tense to react quickly by the time the stroker is ready to shoot at the goal. In that case, just tell the official "no" when asked if you're ready. Then move around and loosen up a bit. Good officials realize that you shouldn't keep any athlete in a ready position for too long. Once you are in a ready position you cannot move until the ball is stroked. Therefore, the referee should explain the penalty stroke to the stroker first, so that you will have to spend less time in the ready position.

your arms and legs a little to relax. Try to visualize the action in advance. Stand on the goal line with your heels touching and shift your stick from hand to hand to measure the extent of your reach. If you

Forward redirects ball into goal. *Photo by Laurie Usher.*

Chapter 8
SCORING

Scoring, the ability to put the ball in the goal, is one of the least understood aspects of field hockey. Why? There are many reasons, not the least of which is the failure of players to frequently and/or properly practice scoring. Even those players who have all the natural scoring qualities—fierce determination, great balance, quick reflexes, perfect timing, anticipation, the instinct to take advantage of sudden opportunities, and being very opportunistic—won't score without practice. Scoring techniques should be perfected during every practice session, specifically during goalkeeping practices and passing drills.

Creating and taking advantage of scoring opportunities can be practiced. A very high percentage of shots completely miss the goal or hit the goalkeeper directly on the pads. Unfortunately, players in scoring position often lose control and wallop the ball as hard as they can. Power is what they go for, but power out of control results in inaccuracy. Finesse and accuracy are the keys to scoring goals. There must be firmness in the shot, to be sure, but a score is a final pass—it goes by the goalkeeper and into the goal. Only shots taken from 12 to 16 yards away from the goal must be powerful as well as accurate.

Field hockey is definitely a team game but at critical moments, when a player is in scoring position, the game becomes a matter of individual performance. When that moment comes, you cannot afford to have any qualms about being selfish or simply hope that the ball will go into the goal. You can only develop the confidence to put the ball in the goal with proper practice, encouragement by the coach, and a strong belief that the whole team benefits from scoring (even if one player does most of it). Whoever scores a goal for your team must realize that all of her teammates have worked together to make that final exciting shot possible.

When the shooter has the time, she should put the ball past the goalkeeper shin-high and on either side of her. It is difficult for the keeper to reach down and stop this kind of shot with her hand or stick and awkward for her to lift her legs up to prevent the goal. A high shot to the corner on the goalkeeper's stick side is very difficult for the goalkeeper to stop without committing a foul. In situations where you're not likely to score with this shot, try it anyway. The goalkeeper will be forced to save the shot, hopefully at full reach, so that a second, follow-up shot may be made successfully off the rebound. The necessary skills for field hockey goal scorers are pushes and flicks, characterized by quick wrist action. Half-hits with very little backswing are also valuable, but no shooter should be so unaware of her surroundings as to have the ball taken away from her during a backswing. Goal scorers should be characterized by, and admired for, their togetherness, compactness, and composure. They should not be known for their flailing arms and legs, unusual noises, or tendency to sprawl in a heap at the feet of the goalkeeper. In fact, good goal scorers make it look easy because they have poise—an awareness of time and space and the exact position of their opponents, especially the goalkeeper.

Developing peripheral vision is particularly important to goal scoring. You must have the ability to see out of the corner of your eye. If you focus on something straight in front of you, you will notice that you can see objects almost at right angles to your line of vision. Cultivate this ability by taking slowly hit balls from the right and left and redirecting them to a predetermined target. This is comparable to taking a pass from a teammate playing a wing position, while watching the goal out of the corner of your eye,

The shooter has put too much power into this shot. A little push or flick to her right and it would have been a sure score. *Photo by Mike Cash.*

and redirecting the ball into a corner past the goalkeeper.

Another important part of scoring is timing. Inside forwards make the great mistake of being in scoring position early and waiting for the ball. They mistakenly sacrifice their mobility. Forwards must lag behind the ball carrier, watching her movements carefully. When the ball carrier swings her stick back to make the cross pass to one of the forwards, the forward should quickly dash toward the ball, beat her defender to it, and then score a goal by getting her stick on the ball and redirecting it into the goal. Forwards who are a little late in making a move will often have a better chance of scoring because their sudden, long reach is unexpected. Never let the ball cross in front of you without playing it, particularly in the striking circle. This is the only excusable situation in which you may lose your balance, reaching so far ahead for a ball that you deflect it into the goal.

Goal scorers need to develop and should be encouraged to develop a cool but aggressive frame of mind. They must learn to convert bad bounces, deflections, and other errors into goals. Never let a ball go over the endline outside of the goal area that could have been kept in play. Scorers are often called lucky, but the truth of the matter is that they make their own luck.

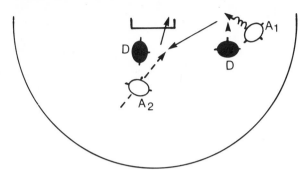

A₂ lags behind A₁ until A₁ moves to pass. A₂ then dashes forward to redirect the ball into the goal for a score. This play is particularly effective on the right side.

SCORING DRILLS

1. Target practice—Set out or draw various targets in the goal or on a wall. Announce which target you are going to hit ahead of time. This forces you to be as accurate as possible. Take your shots at the goal from the following positions: stationary, off a dribble, after beating an opponent, after receiving a pass, and from various angles and distances.
2. Shoot at the goal after practicing combination passing.
3. Practice scoring off badly hit, bouncing balls.
4. One-touch scoring—Redirect or deflect balls from various angles and distances while you are, alternately, stationary and moving.
5. Shoot at the goal while being pressured by a defender—1 on 1, 2 on 2, and 3 on 3. These games can be like schoolyard basketball. Outside the striking circle is the backcourt. If no goalkeeper is available, the goal must be made smaller. The team scoring keeps possession.
6. Practice the following specialized scoring techniques: reverse stick lifts; putting an aerial ball safely into the goal by deflecting it; beating the goalkeeper in a 1 on 1 confrontation; and disguising your pushes and flicks toward the goal.
7. Take full advantage of the goalkeeper's drills by practicing scoring, unless you are given specific instructions to the contrary.

It is vital that you understand the importance of assists in scoring. Assists are passes that lead to goals. Each assist should count as 1 point in the coach's statistics. A particularly good spot from which to assist is the endline (as close to the goal as possible, particularly on the right side). From this position you can make a pass back to your teammate (at a 45° angle) in front of the goal. The relationship between the two of you is the same as that of the supporting player and the ball carrier in midfield. Any time one of your teammates has a better shot at the goal than you do, pass to her—unless you see the goalkeeper moving too soon in anticipation of your pass.

Officials award set plays to one team or the other and check on tie-breaking or overtime procedures. *Photo by Laurie Usher.*

Chapter 9
SET PLAYS

There are many stoppages of play because of boundary violations and fouls. Play is then resumed with one team awarded possession of the ball, and no challenge by the opponent is permitted until the ball is touched. There are a variety of plays, called set plays, that an official can award to one team or the other in order to resume the game. The following discussion of set plays will help you understand how your team can take advantage of, or defend against, these special playing opportunities.

PENALTY CORNER
Attack

The penalty corner is the opportunity for a free shot at the goal. With proper execution, no defender can reach the shooter before the shot. The 3 players needed for a successful penalty corner are a corner pusher or hitter, a handstopper, and a shooter. If the ground is too bumpy then the handstop should be eliminated and

the stick stop used. The rhythm of the play should be push-stop-shoot. Any break in the rhythm and defense can prevent the shot from scoring. Every team should have 2 or 3 variations for use in catching the defense off-guard and for use when the basic penalty corner technique is not working.

The push, rather than a hit, is preferred as the first movement of the penalty corner because the defense cannot tell at what moment the ball will be moved and they cannot see the ball as well. The push must be smooth and accurate. You must keep your eyes on the ball. Lifting the head too soon is a common error. The handstopper will stop the ball by pointing her fingers down, palm facing the oncoming ball, or by pointing her fingers up and smothering the ball with her palm. Your left hand should be used in order to have more of your body out of the way of the shooter. The ball should be stopped about a yard inside the striking circle, so the handstopper must move to the "stop-spot" as the push is made. She must not be moving when she actually stops the ball. After the stop she must back away quickly.

The shooter should be the best hitter on the team, because there is a premium on power as well as accuracy and quickness in hitting. After the push, the ball is stopped opposite the near goalpost and inside the striking circle (to get closer and to have the best angle for the goal—and to allow the shooter to take her shot while she is still moving). A penalty corner should result in a goal being scored. To score a high percentage of goals, the players involved must practice coordinating their movements and maintaining accuracy in their shots. The handstopper and shooter need some agreed upon signal for alternate action when the push is inaccurate or the ball is not pushed hard enough.

Before the penalty corner is taken by your team, your other 3 forwards should move to designated spots on the circle. If the penalty shot fails, one of the forwards may be able to score a goal off the goalkeeper's rebound.

When the defenders have assumed their basic penalty corner positions, a variation in executing the penalty corner will often confuse the defenders and result in a goal being scored. The designated shooter can pass left to the pusher (who moves toward goal after her push) or right to the teammate on her weak side. When executing a variation on the basic penalty corner, the players, particularly the pusher, must not signal their intentions by altering any of their motions. The basic penalty corner should be taken on

Handstopper and shooter prepare to execute a penalty corner. When done properly, there is ample time to shoot.

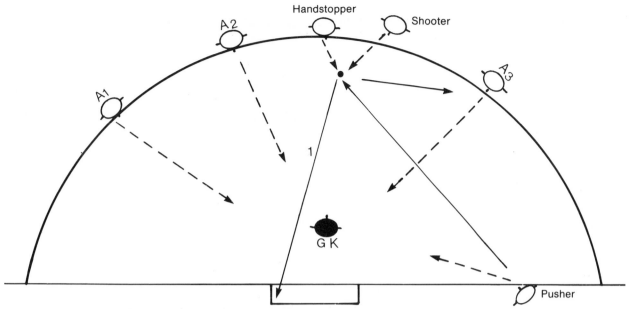

Offensive Penalty Corner. A_1, A_2, and A_3 are positioned to receive the goalkeeper's rebound.

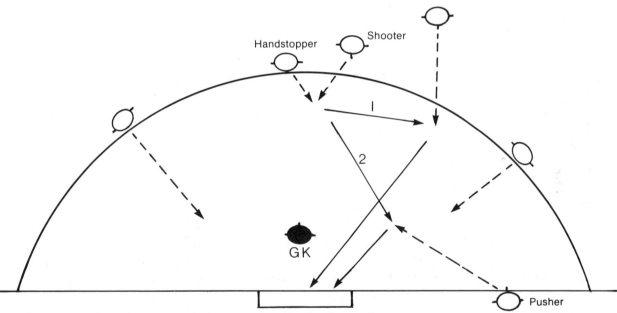

Variation 1 or 2 may lead to a goal when executing the offensive penalty corner.

the left because it is more difficult for the opposition to defend. Attackers who understand penetration and mobility will and should force penalty corners to be awarded to them when they aren't successful in getting the shots they want in the normal flow of play. The attacker's primary objective is to score a goal. If the shot is not successful, the objective becomes to be awarded a penalty corner.

Defense

The best defense against a penalty corner is to avoid having one awarded to the other team. Keeping the ball out of the striking circle is the best method. If play does move into the striking circle, defenders must have and maintain good defensive positions. Anticipating a pass and intercepting the ball before an attacker arrives will help you to avoid giving up a

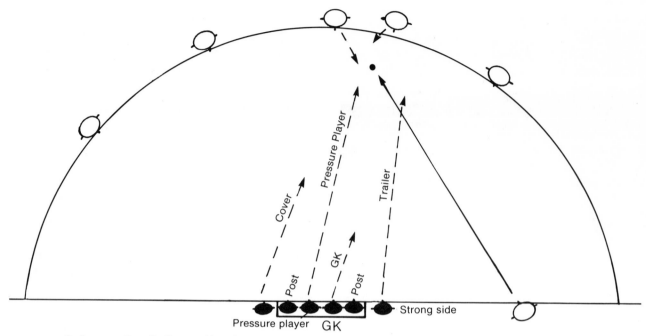

Defense on Penalty Corner. Note the open corridor in front of the goalkeeper so that she can see and no one is in position to become injured.

penalty corner. However, defenders must always be prepared to stop or disrupt the opposition's execution of the basic penalty corner and its variations. If they can't stop the shot they must be prepared to clear any rebounds off their own goalkeeper. The defending team has 6 players to work with. First, the goalkeeper must step out 4 to 5 yards in front of the goal line to narrow the shooting angle. The goalkeeper could move out even farther in front of the goal to narrow the shooting angle even more. However, if the goalkeeper comes out too far, one successful pass by the attacking team would put her so far from the goal that she would not be able to recover. No matter where the goalkeeper stands she must be stationary when the shot is actually made.

Two defenders should be stationed in the goal just inside the goalposts. Their job is to stop any shot that passes by the goalkeeper. These defenders should exhibit courage and determination as well as technical skills. Each of these defenders should stand with legs together, and the

stick should rest on the ground in front of her feet. If no shot is made, both of the defenders in the goal should immediately run out of the goal to pick up the nearest attacker or to play the ball. Once the shot is made, the defenders in the goal should go after the ball. They should not just stand in the goal waiting for the ball to come to them.

The fourth defender is called the pressure player. Her job is to rush the ball in an attempt to force the shooter to make a hasty and inaccurate shot at the goal. The pressure player rushes out from the left of the goalkeeper (so as not to block the keeper's view of the ball). The pressure player should keep her body to the left of the shot to avoid injuring herself, and she should carry her stick firmly in her right hand with the stickhead on the ground in the path of the shot. A fifth, strong side (ballside) defender should be prepared to intercept a pass to the shooter's left or to pick up the shooter if the pressure player has managed to slow her down. This defender is often called the trailer. The

The pressure player and trailer put pressure on penalty corner shooter. Keeper has clear view of ball.

because the ball is farther from the goal. Since the ball must travel farther, the defense has more time to stop it. Like the penalty corner, the long corner requires 3 players to execute the play. Unlike the penalty corner, the long corner begins with a player hitting (not pushing) the ball. The second player both stops the ball and shoots it toward the goal. The sequence of play is hit-stop-shoot. Your team should start the long corner with its best hitter, so the ball can reach your shooter before a defender does. Much of the success of a long corner depends on the same factors as success with a penalty corner. One variation of the long corner is to have one of your teammates level with and about 5 yards away from the hitter. Your teammate can receive a pass from the hitter and, although your teammate is not in a position to shoot for the goal, she can set up a scoring play with a pass into the circle.

sixth player is the covering player. She is positioned outside the goal to the keeper's left. She comes out about seven yards to play the keeper's rebound or any loose ball, or to intercept a pass on her left.

LONG CORNER

Attack

The long corner is not as advantageous to the attacking team as the penalty corner

Defense

If a basic long corner is taken, the defense

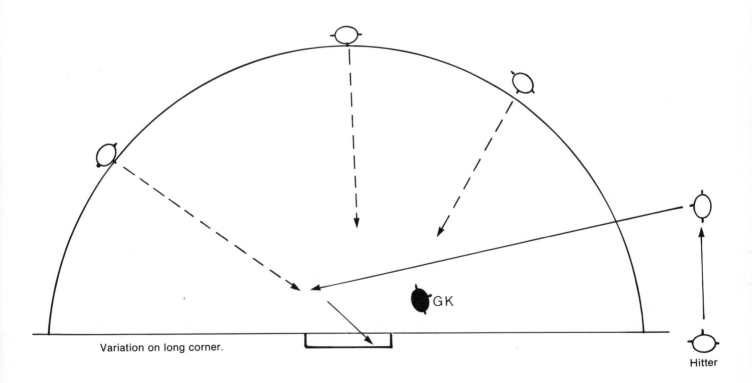

Variation on long corner.

GK

Hitter

is the same as the penalty corner, except that the strong side defender should be a little wider. If the short pass is made, the strong side defender should run on a line toward the receiver but must not charge at the player in control of the ball outside the striking circle. The pressure player should move out to the striking circle's edge, ready to play any ball in that direction. The near goalpost defender must run out to cover the strong side defender, and the weak side defender should move out to a position where she can play a goalkeeper's rebound or else cross-pass. The other goalpost player should play the goalpost basically the same as she would for a penalty corner. However, she must be ready to run out of the goal if the ball suddenly shifts to the weak side.

FREE HIT

An official may award a free hit to a team to compensate that team for any of a wide variety of fouls committed by the opposing team. When a free hit is awarded because of a foul committed inside the striking circle, it takes the form of a penalty corner. But when a free hit is awarded for a foul committed outside the striking circle, it is taken from the spot where the breach was committed. No player may remain within 5 yards of the player taking the free hit. A free hit often helps a team sustain its midfield attack. In the attack area near the striking circle, a free hit can result in a shot at the goal. In the defense area of the field, a free hit can relieve the pressure of your opponents' tactics.

Attack

Almost every player will stop concentrating as soon as the whistle blows. To execute a free hit properly you must move quickly and decisively: Check the position of the players on the field, place the ball on the spot where the foul was committed, and make your pass. You should pass forward to one of your teammates if she is free and if the pass will catch the defense napping. Otherwise, make a lateral pass or pass back to one of your teammates. Whatever you do, don't hesitate! Your receiver has the option to dribble the ball, so you should quickly pass to whichever teammate can most easily evade her defenders.

Defense

The defenders must read the situation quickly and, without hesitation, run into their proper positions while remaining constantly aware of the position of the ball and the players around them. Defending forwards can be valuable if they are alert and anticipate the direction in which the ball will move. Should a forward get the ball, particularly from a lateral or back pass, she will probably have a chance to counterattack because her opponents will be outnumbered and/or disorganized.

PUSH-IN

On a sideline boundary violation the ball is put in play by a push. The rules make this very difficult. With the opponents only 5 yards away and the pusher not allowed to lift or hit the ball, successful execution of the push-in is difficult. When the push-in can be taken quickly it has the best chance for success.

It is very easy for the defending team to intercept the ball on a push-in. The push-in is taken from a sideline, with the defenders forming a semicircle around the player executing the push-in. Pushing forward along the sideline may result in your team's loss of ball possession, but your defense will have time to organize while your forwards try to recapture the ball. Making a lateral or back push-in is very dangerous because the other team has a chance to intercept the ball deep inside your defending area. If you are going to make a lateral or back push-in, you must be certain that your teammate will receive it. One of your team's wingbacks should normally make the push-in. When the push-in occurs deep within the attack area, however, one of your wings should make it. When making a push-in try to pass to one of your teammates who is moving between her opponents. Be careful, though, not to take any risks if you are making a push-in from your own end of the field. A clever defender will often deliberately leave you the space to make a lateral or back push-in. But once the ball is in motion the defender will immediately move to intercept it. That sort of play will give the other team possession of the ball with counterattack possibilities.

PENALTY STROKE

A penalty stroke is awarded to the attacking team for a foul that prevented a goal and was committed by the defending team within its own striking circle. The stroke is taken from a point 7 yards in front of the center of the goal. The defensive tactics of the goalkeeper during a penalty stroke have already been discussed in the chapter on goalkeeping.

Who is under more pressure, the goalkeeper or the stroker? Many say the keeper but I disagree. A mentally well-prepared goalkeeper knows she will lose every well-placed penalty stroke and prepares herself to save those that are inaccurate and/or mishit. The attacker can only fail through lack of practice.

Power and accuracy are essential to a good penalty stroke. Since hitting is not permitted, the flick is most popular because it can be elevated off the ground. The areas to shoot for are the corners of the goal—high and low. If the keeper is short, high flicks to the corners will be out of her reach and if she is tall, shots at the height of her shins are awkward for her to get to. If the keeper has her stick in one hand then your ideal target is high on her stick side, because she'll have to raise her stick above her shoulder (thereby committing a foul) to stop the ball. You can stay within the rules governing the penalty stroke and still try to fool the goalkeeper with deceptive movements of your eyes and body, or a quick snap of your wrist. But losing the chance to score on a penalty stroke because you don't know the rules is inexcusable. Not waiting for the official's signal, excessive delay after the whistle, or taking more than one step are common errors that strokers make. Finally, every team should have two specialists in taking penalty strokes and, in leagues where ties are broken by penalty strokes, each team must have 5 strokers.

Penalty stroke.

Proper training to develop overall body strength, flexibility, and endurance really pays off during the game. *Photo by Laurie Usher.*

Chapter 10
FITNESS

No one can argue that field hockey can be played better and more easily when the players have stamina, strength, and quickness. Players run 3 to 5 miles in a 70-minute game. They do frequent sprints, punctuated with changes of direction, twists, turns, and reaches. The proper execution of field hockey techniques requires the use of a strong back and strong hands, wrists, arms, shoulders, buttocks, and legs. All of these parts of the body can be significantly improved through a proper training program. There is no excuse for any coach to be fooled by the age-old myths about developing bulging muscles. Women simply do not have the hormonal capacity to develop such musculature. One look at Karen Shelton, Chris Evert, Ann Meyers, and Francie Larrieu, all world-class performers in field hockey, tennis, basketball, and track, respectively, and you can safely conclude that training is very positive and enhances a player's appearance. Strong muscles don't have to be big muscles. Jack Wilmore, who has worked extensively with women athletes, says "women have increased their strength as much as 44% with almost no increase in muscle size."

Most women athletes and coaches are afraid of breaking out of the cultural stereotype of the "gentler sex." It takes courage to make the psychological commitment to serious competition and to the conditioning that is required to adapt to the physical stresses of field hockey. Ridicule and hassling, particularly by men, is something that you have to live with for a while—in the weight room and on the track. Derisive remarks turn into genuine respect in a short time when others see the serious and knowledgeable commitment you are making to the sport. Only losers fail to realize that fitness (like sports in general) is a two-sex activity.

Your motivation to train must be your desire to perform up to your capacity throughout every game, all season long. A player who is not in shape begins to focus on her tiredness, she no longer executes the techniques of field hockey efficiently, and she does not try for balls that are within her reach. She makes excuses, "I thought Susie was going to get it!" Like a dieter who imagines herself thin, the field hockey player trains because she imagines herself performing and moving with confidence during the entire game. She knows she doesn't have to "save" herself for the last 10 minutes. There is no doubt that training is by far the least enjoyable activity in field hockey, but winning players cannot neglect their training!

Physical conditioning is divided into endurance, speed, strength, and flexibility. The following descriptions and programs are a "starter" set. There are many good fitness books available, and all colleges and universities (and many high schools) are fairly well staffed with athletic trainers. It has been my experience that trainers have been most interested and cooperative because they realize the problem facing women in sports. However, the coaches and players must take the initiative in seeking good training.

ENDURANCE

Heart and lung efficiency is necessary to run continuously for extended periods of time. This endurance is built up over long periods of time before the season begins and is the basis for effective speed work. January through June is the time to begin building endurance, since most field hockey seasons begin in the autumn. For those just beginning an endurance program it is important not to think about speed.

The beginner must build a basis for endurance by first running and walking a certain number of minutes. If you start out doing speed and distance work you will physically break down. Your beginning goal should be to be able to run consistently for 40 to 45 minutes with no consideration for how far or how fast you are running. You should begin working toward your goal by first running for 12 minutes at a time. If you can't run the full time you should walk a while. When you can run comfortably for 12 minutes it's time to move on and gradually increase the time you run to develop endurance. A four-day-per-week program would look like this:

Table 1   Four-Day-Per-Week Running Program (in minutes)

	Weeks 1 & 2	Weeks 3 & 4	Weeks 5 & 6	Weeks 7 & 8
Day 1	15–20	20–25	25–30	30–35
Day 2	15–20	20–25	25–30	30–35
Day 3	Rest	Rest	Rest	Rest
Day 4	20–25	25–30	30–35	35–40
Day 5	Rest	Rest	Rest	Rest
Day 6	20–25	25–30	30–35	35–40
Day 7	Rest	Rest	Rest	Rest

Once you have reached this plateau, you must make even greater demands of yourself. You must tell your body to run farther and/or faster. The best measure for cardiovascular fitness is the pulse. A well-conditioned athlete will have a resting pulse of from 50 to 60 beats per minute. To attain this, your heart and lungs must work so that your pulse is pushed up to 170 to 180 beats per minute. Immediately after a workout the player should take her pulse in her neck by counting the beats for 15 seconds and multiplying by four. If your pulse is not high enough, you must run faster and/or farther. With experience you will know how hard your body is working and will only have to make periodic pulse checks. The following is a good, progressive endurance program using the "infallible" pulse for measuring the work load. This method makes each player an individual who is only competing against herself to get into shape.

However, if you have to alter your running motion by limping or making any other bodily changes because of pain then you should cut back your speed or distance. If that doesn't work, stop and rest a few days. Even so, you must endure and expect discomfort and stagnant periods when you'll "guts" your way through. The tendency to rationalize and make excuses is great but you must not give in. As Fred Shero, coach of the two-time Stanley Cup Champion Philadelphia Flyers, said, "Train without pain and you train in vain!" Winners do the things that losers don't like to do! Where you choose to run is your business. Some players like the routine and ease that a track provides while others take to the roads, the woods, or the beach. You must have training shoes that fit well and will absorb the shock of continuous running. This may be a bit hard on your pocketbook but good shoes are well worth the expense.

Table 2 Progressive Endurance Program (miles per day)

	10-Mile Week	18-Mile Week	25-Mile Week
Day 1 Medium	1½	3	4
Day 2 Light	½	1½	2½
Day 3 Heavy	2½	4	6
Day 4 Light	½	1½	2½
Day 5 Medium	1½	3	4
Day 6 Heavy	3½	5	6
Day 7 Rest	—	—	—

Step up your program when your body is ready. Doing too much will cause you unusual discomfort and pain resulting in a physical breakdown. The line between unusual discomfort and normal, expected discomfort is not the easiest to describe.

SPEED

Speed is not as important as your ability to start quickly (or explode off the mark) and your agility in changing your direction. Speed work will be ineffective and futile if you have no endurance. About 6 weeks before the first team practice a player with well-developed endurance should alternate days of interval speed work with days of endurance work. The purpose of these speed workouts is to prepare you for the frequent short bursts of speed and changes of direction that you execute in the course of a field hockey game. If you are not in good physical condition you will simply not be able to do these things consistently—probably not at all late in the game. Squabbling, hassling, and excuse-making by players in games and practices can often be traced directly to lack of conditioning. You can't move effectively when you are tired and/or sore, and it is easier to point a finger at someone else and make excuses for yourself than to admit the truth. Your general running program for the 6 weeks prior to the opening practice should be as follows:

Day 1   Light Run
Day 2   Interval Speed Work
Day 3   Heavy Run
Day 4   Interval Speed Work
Day 5   Medium Run
Day 6   Interval Speed Work
Day 7   Rest

When doing speed work again take your pulse to measure your efficiency. Each sprint interval should take your pulse up to 170 to 180 beats per minute. In the beginning, your speed for each of the sprint distances should be 1 to 2 seconds slower than your fastest time for that distance. On each speed work day you will do a group of sprints or work intervals called a set. Each sprint within the set is the work interval, called a repetition or "rep" for short. Between each repetition there is a rest interval which is

3 times the length of the work interval. So if you sprint 55 yards in 7 seconds you will rest 21 seconds before doing the next rep. The rest between sets is the time it takes your pulse to return to 120 to 130 beats per minute. During the rest interval between reps you can walk, stretch, or jog. Do the following speed program, which totals 1½ miles, 3 times a week for 6 weeks:

Sets	Reps	Distance
1	4	220 yards
1	8	110 yards
2	8	55 yards

As you feel yourself getting stronger (using your pulse as an indicator) run each rep a little faster and/or work a little harder by jogging instead of walking during the rest interval. Each rep should be close in time to the rep preceding it. Someone running 7-second 55s might have reps reading 8, 10, 9, 8, 10, 9, 9, and 9 seconds. The starts should be practical in terms of field hockey, not track. Here are some moves for you to try when you are performing reps of 55 yards each: Take 3 or 4 jogging steps toward, lateral to, and exactly opposite your line of sprint; run backwards and then turn for the start of your sprint; and start your sprint from the stance of a defender on the endline during a penalty corner. It is very important for you to .develop an explosive start when you sprint. Goalkeepers do not need the same endurance program as other players, but they must not neglect to work on their endurance. Actually, quickness is the most important quality for a goalkeeper. Keepers should do some very short sprints from lying-on-the-ground starts, because they must be able to get up from the ground quickly to make saves.

If you stick to this sensible endurance and speed program, you will be able to perform every coach's favorite testing device—the 12-minute run. You will not only be able to do it but you will not be laboring during your run, you will finish strong, and you will be able to participate in normal practices without undo discomfort. Running 1¾ miles in 12 minutes is a very good performance and college and club players with natural speed who work hard on conditioning can do 1⅞ to 2 miles in that time. Players who run less than 1½ miles in 12 minutes either have "suspect" natural speed or didn't work at their conditioning program. In the former case these players can often overcome their lack of natural speed and quickness by being smart. By knowing their limitations and playing within their own abilities, they learn to always be in the right place at the right time.

STRENGTH

After studying the mechanics of strength-building techniques and the parts of the body that benefit from those techniques, it will be obvious how much more efficient you can be with strength training. A field hockey player who is strong is better than a weak player. Your weight-training program should be started at the same time as your speed work, but your weight training should be done on the days you are running. For maximum results you must lift a weight from 8 to 12 times. If you can't lift it 8 times, it's too heavy and if you can lift it more than 12 times, it's too light. For some reason one of the biggest problems you'll face is deciding what weight to start with. Before your first serious lift, you must practice the proper technique of the lift, and *then* experiment to find the right starting weight. Players should do 2 sets of the following exercises, but complete all of them before starting your second set. Keep lifting each weight until you can lift it 13 times, then increase the weight, and start with 8 reps again. The following exercises should be done in order:

Leg Press—(Universal Gym Quads, buttocks): Sit with your feet on the pedals. Grasp the side of the seat with your hands. Fully extend your legs, pause, and recover to the starting position. Do not let your buttocks come off the seat and don't let your legs lock straight out.

Leg Extension (Leg Extension Machine—Quads): Sit on the machine, lean back slightly, and grasp the side of machine. After hooking your feet under the rollers, extend your legs completely, pause, and return. Keep your buttocks on the seat.

Leg Curl (Leg Curl Machine—hamstrings): Lie face down on the machine with your heels hooked under the rollers and your knees just off the edge of the bench. Flex your legs until your calves are at right angles to your body, pause, and recover.

Heel Raise (Barbell—calves): Stand with the barbell across your shoulders and your toes elevated on a board. Raise your heels as high as possible off the floor until you are up on your toes, pause, and slowly recover.

Bench Press (Barbells or Universal Gym—pectorals, deltoids, triceps): Lie face up on the bench with your knees bent and your feet on the floor. Your buttocks and shoulder blades should be in contact with the bench. Hold the barbell with your arms extended. Lower the barbell to your chest, pause, and return. Don't arch your back.

Lat Pulldown (Lat Machine—latissimis dorsi, biceps): Kneel or sit using an underhand and shoulder-width grip to grasp the bar. Pull the bar down and back to your upper chest, pause, and return.

Upright Row (Barbell—deltoids, biceps, trapezius: Stand with your arms hanging down with the barbell in both your hands and held less than shoulder width apart. Pull the barbell up to your chin, pause, and return. Stand straight. Don't bend at the waist.

Side Lateral Raises (Dumbbells—deltoids): Keep your arms at your sides with a dumbbell in each hand. Your palms should be facing your body. Bend your body slightly forward at the waist. Raise the dumbbells sideward and upward until they are level with your ears, pause, and recover.

Triceps Extension (Lat Machine—triceps): Stand facing the bar which you have pulled down to your neck level. Use an overhand grip on the bar with your elbows touching your rib cage. Using only your lower arms, pull the bar down until your arms are extended, pause, and return. Keep your elbows in and don't bend at the waist.

Biceps Curl (Barbell—biceps): Extend your arms straight down with hands holding the bar with an underhand grip. Raise the barbell forward and upward to your chin, pause, and return. Keep your elbows down and in. Don't lean back.

Wrist Curls (Barbell—forearm flexors): Sit with your forearms resting on your thighs and the backs of your hands against your knees. Lift the barbell upward and forward, pause, and return. Keep your forearms and elbows on your thighs and lift the barbell by flexing your wrists only.

Reverse Wrist Curls (Barbells—forearm extensors): The same as wrist curls, except your palms are down.

Sit-Ups (hip flexors, quads, abdominals): Sit on the floor with your feet close to your buttocks, your knees together, your hands interlocked behind your head, your buttocks slightly elevated, and your upper body slightly inclined backward. Lower your body, but don't let your back touch the floor, pause, and return. Make your muscles work by doing sit-ups slowly—4 seconds to raise your body and 8 seconds to lower it. The higher your hips the greater the difficulty.

Squeezing a Rubber Ball (hand flexors): Do this while you're watching television!

These are good basic exercises for your legs, body, arms, and hands. There are many other exercises that can be done for variation, depending on the availability of equipment. Many authorities believe the Nautilus is the best machine because it can exercise the full range of your muscular motion and because your workout is shorter. In all but the last 2 exercises the weight should be moved in 2 seconds and, after a slight pause, it should be returned in 4 seconds.

FLEXIBILITY

This refers to the range of motion that is possible at a joint. In field hockey where a player is running and at the same time reaching, twisting, pushing, and going through other body contortions, she can increase her efficiency and lessen the chances of muscle and joint injuries by incorporating flexibility exercises into her warm-up. Each player is different, so you

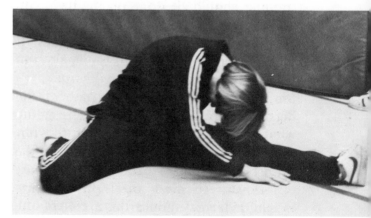

Stretching out! A good, strong stretch is relaxing.

Doing flexibility exercises allows players like the one on the right to make reaches like this without pulling muscles.

should not engage in a flexibility competition with your teammates. Each stretch should be static, not bobbing, and held for about 30 seconds. Perhaps the most important aspect of stretching is knowing the difference between a good stretch and pain. A good, strong stretch is relaxing—reach too far and it hurts and is not relaxing. By reaching far enough but not too far, you will experience a noticeable improvement in a relatively short time. Toe touches, body twists, arm circles and crosses, hurdle sitting, the plow, Indian curls, shoulder stands, and wall stretches are excellent, well-known stretches.

Conditioning alone does not make the game, but the game deteriorates without it. Young players, junior high and younger, should not indulge in great training programs but should work on techniques and individual and group tactics. Senior high, college, and club athletes who want to be good, competitive field hockey players must work out in the off-season and must avoid any long periods of inactivity. A yearly program would look like this:

Pre-Season, Phase I

(6 weeks prior to opening of practice)

Start a maximum-effort program to build your endurance, speed, and strength.

Pre-Season, Phase II

(1 to 2 weeks prior to opening of school)

This is usually when players go to hockey camp and/or practice for a week prior to the opening of school. Your program for the day should be:

Morning (2½ to 3 hours)

Do your warm-up, creative dribbling, techniques practice, goalkeeping practice, and pressure drills when you've mastered your techniques.

Afternoon (1½ hours)

Do your warm-up, then practice individual and group tactics with the goalkeeper.

Evening (1½ hours)

Do your warm-up, then practice team tactics on both the half and full field. (¼ hour)

Sprint 3 times a week and practice other interval training with your stick and ball on half the field.

In-Season

(September through November)

Practices and games. Each practice should last about 2 hours, until the season is about two-thirds over. After that, each practice should last from 1¼ to 1½ hours.

Post-Season

(December)

Rest.

(January through June)

Maintain or increase your endurance and strength. Play some other sports—racquetball, squash, basketball, cross-country skiing, and indoor field hockey.

glossary

Back pass: Pass to a player behind you.

Ball control: Maneuvering or maintaining possession of the ball.

Beat: Moving the ball past an•opponent; eliminating an opponent.

Center: Pass from the outside of the field to the middle of the field.

Center forward: Middle player on forward line of traditional formation.

Clear: Removing the ball from the scoring area.

Combination defense: Some players playing zone defense and some playing man-to-man defense.

Concentration: The deliberate and controlled focus on one object, task, or line of thought.

Counterattack: Beginning an attack immediately after gaining possession of the ball.

Cover: Defender stationed between a teammate and opponent challenging for the ball so that she will be in position should her teammate be beaten.

Cross pass: Pass from one side of the field to the other.

Defender: A player whose major contributions are to get the ball from her opponents, and to prevent her opponents from scoring.

Defense: The team without the ball.

Depth: (1) *Defense:* Players back each other up along the length of the field.

(2) *Offense:* Players without the ball are either ahead of or in back of the ball, giving length to the attack.

Diagonal pass: Pass to a player diagonally across the field.

Dodge: See **Beat.**

Dribble: Individual technique of moving and maintaining control of the ball with short taps off the end of the stick.

Drive: See **Hit.**

Fake: Giving a pretense of moving, hitting, or pushing in one direction only to quickly change direction.

Fielding: Slowing the ball's speed with the end of the stick so that the ball is immediately under control.

First time: One time; one touch.

Flick: Push that is lofted, primarily a shot; getting the ball out of danger.

Formation: Same as system.

Forwards: Primarily offense, the first line of the attack.

Fullbacks or backs: The last line of defense.

Give and go: Pass in front of opponent to teammate who immediately returns the ball behind the opponent.

Goal: (1) The unit of scoring; (2) the cage on the endline into which a team tries to put the ball.

Goalkeeper: The specially equipped player who protects the goal and has privileges not afforded other players.

Halfbacks or halves: Midfield players who have attacking as well as defending responsibilities; also called links or midfielders.

Hit: Stroke used for moving the ball over great distances and for shooting.

Influence: A defender positioning herself on an angle to her opponent such that she forces the opponent to move in one given direction.

Inners or insides: Middle forwards, primary scorers; also called strikers.

Interception: Getting the ball before it reaches the intended receiver.

Lead pass: Pass aimed ahead of the receiver so she can pick it up without breaking stride.

Links: Halves, midfielders.

Long game: Game that features passes of more than 15 yards.

Man-to-man: Defender is responsible for one player and follows her regardless of the player's field position.

Marking: Defender playing close enough to an opponent to prevent the opponent from receiving a pass; (2) defender playing close enough to tackle and/or pressure an opponent immediately upon receiving the ball; (3) man-to-man defense.

Narrowing the angle: Goalkeeper coming off the goal line to reduce the possibilities of a good shot. When the goalkeeper comes off the goal line the shooter sees more of the goalkeeper than the goal.

Numerical superiority: More attack players than defense players in the vicinity of the ball.

Overlap: Attacking run by a defender who comes from behind, passing her wing on the outside.

Pace: Hitting the ball hard enough to get past an opponent but not so hard as to pass beyond the intended receiver.

Pass: Intentionally moving the ball from one teammate to another.

Penetration: Quickly and accurately moving the ball via a dribble or pass into scoring position.

Playing distance: The distance (about the length of the body stretched well forward plus the length of the stick) between the defender and her opponent with the ball. Playing distance gives the player with the ball space to maneuver.

Poise: (1) Awareness of time and space and the positioning of teammates and opponents; (2) awareness of when to emphasize power and when to emphasize accuracy; (3) remaining calm under pressure.

Pressure: Decreasing the time and space that an attacking player has in which to pass or dribble.

Push: The stroke used for short passes, with no preliminary action prior to release, making it the quickest pass.

Retreat: Defender giving ground to a dribbler, waiting for the right moment to tackle.

Reverse stick: Playing the ball with the toe of the stick down.

Run for cover: A beaten defender making a direct path to the goal, positioning herself to cover a teammate challenging for the ball or to contain an opponent.

Save: Preventing a goal, usually accomplished by the goalkeeper.

Scissors: Diagonal move by teammates; one player has the ball and her teammate is behind her.

Score: (1) Goal; (2) The final pass.

Set plays: Corners, free hits, push-ins—situations where no pressure, or limited pressure, can be exerted.

Short game: Game that features passes of less than 15 yards.

Square: Pass that moves parallel to the endline.

Striker: Inside forward whose main job is scoring goals.

Strong side: Side the ball is on, the player's right side.

Support: Coming from behind to establish numerical superiority in the vicinity of the ball; 2 on 1.

Sweeper: Free defender who covers and roams behind the defense, picking up all through passes, and who must take on a forward who breaks free with the ball.

System: The arrangement of players on the field.

Tackling: Taking on an opponent with the ball to gain possession of it.

Tactics: (1) The mental aspect of play, the outwitting of opponents; (2) short-range objectives which change from game to game and player to player.

Through pass: Pass that moves parallel to the sideline and through opponents.

Timing: (1) Releasing a pass at the right moment in relation to the positions of teammates and opponents; (2) player without the ball moving at the right time.

Transiton: Changing from offense to defense or vice versa.

Weak side: (1) The left side of the player; (2) the side of the field away from the ball.

Width: Players taking a wide position toward the sideline.

Wings or outsides: Two forwards on the extreme outside of the attacking players.

Wingbacks: Fullbacks who play the flanks.

Zigzag dribble: Controlling ball in front of the body and propelling it forward in a zigzag pattern. The ball is moved alternately with forehand and reverse stick movements.

Zone: Players play in an area and defend against any opponent who comes into that area.